CW00369751

The Murder of Rachel Nickell

The Murder of Rachel Nickell

Mike Fielding

BLAKE'S
TRUE
CRIME
LIBRARY

Published by Blake Publishing Ltd,
3 Bramber Court, 2 Bramber Road,
London W14 9PB, England

First published in paperback 2000

ISBN 1 85782 338 9

British Library Cataloguing-in-Publication Data:

A catalogue record for this book is
available from the British Library.

Typeset by t2

Printed in Finland by
WS Bookwell, Juva

1 3 5 7 9 10 8 6 4 2

Dear Reader,

You are about to read of one of the most devastating crimes ever to have taken place in this country. Not only was Rachel Nickell brutally attacked and murdered on Wimbledon Common in broad daylight in 1992, but the crime was also tragically witnessed by her two-year-old son.

In this probing book, Mike Fielder goes deep into the investigation that tried to find the sick person responsible for this crime. He reveals the strange life of the prime suspect Colin Stagg, including his family background, his solitary life with only his dog for company and his allegiance to the pagan cult of Wicca.

Stagg was not convicted of the crime and is now a free man. The case was thrown out of court, with the police evidence being deemed inadmissable. Will the murderer ever be apprehended or will this remain yet another unclosed police file? Read the facts and decide for yourself...

Adam Parfitt
Editor
Blake's True Crime Library

Contents

Prologue

Today, after being found not guilty of the murder of Rachel Nickell on Wimbledon Common, Colin Stagg is a free man. He is free to enjoy the tranquillity of the common with his dog Brandy and the new love of his life, Diane Rooney. He is seeking to claim enormous damages from the police after the evidence of an undercover policewoman, who was involved in a 'honey trap', was thrown out by an Old Bailey judge and the operation branded 'reprehensible'.

Author Mike Fielder was among the first journalists to arrive at Wimbledon Common on 15 July 1992 after Rachel had been found murdered under a silver birch tree, her two-year-old son clutching her ravaged body. Fielder has followed every twist and turn of this remarkable story ever since. He tells why the police became so certain that loner Cohn Stagg was the man who had killed Rachel Nickell, how they asked a pretty young policewoman to befriend him to try to prove his guilt, how they ventured into the bizarre world of witchcraft and the black arts seeking a solution to this frightening crime, and how, two years and two months later, it all fell apart inside the Old Bailey's Court Number One.

For 23 years a crime reporter on *The Sun*, Fielder has covered stories worldwide, from the Costa del

Crime to the SAS shooting of IRA terrorists in Gibraltar and the cannibal killings of Jeffrey Dahmer in Milwaukee. He believes that, until then, none had generated as much emotional turbulence throughout the whole of Britain as the dreadful murder of Rachel Nickell. It is the crime everyone remembers. The crime that sent shudders of fear through the nation. Here, for the first time, he gives the evidence an Old Bailey jury would have heard if Mr Justice Ognall had allowed the case to go ahead. This book does not seek to challenge either the acquittal of Stagg or the unique investigative methods of the Wimbledon murder squad. Its aim is to provide a factual account of the circumstances surrounding the arrest of Stagg and the unprecedented problems faced by the police officers investigating the murder. It goes behind the life and times of Colin Stagg and examines the shattering effect upon Rachel's family. Fielder, who himself has a 23-year-old daughter, the same age as Rachel Nickell when she died, believes that this tragedy without end is sure to surface again and again until we know for sure who was the killer on the common that fateful day.

A Cruel End

Mike Wickerson's face said it all. Something quite dreadful had happened in Windmill Wood; something way beyond the bounds of his 26 years' police experience. The detective chief inspector was feeling raw pain and was not ashamed to show it.

He walked slowly from the leafy copse on Wimbledon Common on that sunny July day in 1992 and his voice was charged with emotion as he faced newspaper reporters and television crews with the first details of a murder that was to horrify the nation. His head shook slowly from side to side, as if in disbelief at what he had seen, as he stepped over the red and white police incident tapes and dug deep for the right words. 'She was just an innocent young mother walking her little boy in a public park . . . it's quite horrific . . . so tragic.'

Wickerson couldn't say he had witnessed the work of the devil that day — it's not in the police directory of crimes — but that surely was the reality of the situation. He had seen the crumpled body of lovely Rachel Nickell lying at the foot of a silver birch tree, mutilated by a mass of frenzied stab wounds; she had been almost decapitated by the ferocity of the attack. Her blue jeans and panties had been pulled down around her ankles and she had been sexually abused. It was a shocking, senseless murder in any circumstances. What made it so heartwrenchingly tragic was the fact that Rachel's tiny son Alex had seen every detail of the madman's assault. The little boy, not quite three years old at the time, was found caked in his mother's blood, clinging to her body, pleading, 'Get up, Mummy, get up.' They were the last words Alex spoke for more than 24 hours. The monstrous attack left him speechless with terror. Police could only imagine the effect on the toddler's mind, the nightmare he must have suffered as he pleaded with frightened eyes for the killer to stop, the agony as he clutched Rachel's body while her life ebbed away. It was hardly surprising that there were tears from case-hardened officers as the enormity of the Rachel Nickell murder sank in.

It was a case which was to tax the full resources of Scotland Yard for another thirteen months and take detectives into previously uncharted territory in a remarkable investigation intended to snare the man they believed had butchered Rachel so callously.

The killing sent shudders through every young woman in Britain, through every parent with a young daughter. How could this happen in one of the capital's most prestigious parks, a green oasis in suburban south-west London, regularly patrolled by mounted rangers and used by hundreds of people daily, from joggers and riders to golfers, picnickers and fresh-air fanatics? Veteran detective John Bassett, an officer with an impressive track record in major crimes, was given the task of spearheading the inquiry, backed by Mike Wickerson and a 40-strong team of the best officers available, operating from an incident room at Wimbledon police station. From the outset it was clear that this was destined to be one of the most important investigations ever undertaken by Scotland Yard. It was of particular and personal concern to the then Commissioner of the Metropolitan Police, Sir Peter Imbert. The normally affable Scotland Yard boss lived within a stone's throw of the common and his wife was among the regulars who strolled its paths and woodlands.

Rachel's body, curled almost in a foetal position, was discovered by retired architect Michael Murray as he walked his dog along a path which snaked across the 1,100-acre common, past the landmark windmill with its giant white sails, and dipped down into a copse of young oaks and birches. It was a warm and sunny day — temperature a pleasant 65 degrees — and Mr Murray thought at first he had stumbled on a young lady sunbathing. The sickening reality of the situation hit him as he neared the prostrate figure, lying a few yards off the path. He could see it was a half-naked woman, clearly dead, grotesquely injured, with a bewildered little boy gripping tightly to her arm and a little black mongrel dog whimpering nearby. Murray reached out to help the youngster but so tight was his grip on his mother's arm that Murray had to prise the little boy's fingers gently free before he would let go. Murray lifted the boy into his arms, handed him urgently to two women walking nearby and then dashed to the park rangers' office, some 300 yards away, to alert the police.

It was 10:35 a.m. on 15 July 1992 and Rachel Nickell, 23 years old, a devoted and caring mother, happily settled in a loving long-term relationship with Alex's father and with every expectation of a future full of happiness, had become a murder statistic. It was a cruel end for a girl whose golden hair and model looks regularly turned heads and whose bright, almost toothy, smile gave her an endearing air of innocence.

Detective Superintendent Bassett and his team knew at once that they were looking for a maniac so depraved that he would almost certainly kill again if he were not quickly captured. Rachel's body bore all the hallmarks of a demonic attack — 49 stab wounds which had damaged every vital organ in her body. Any one of a dozen individual wounds would have killed her. The savagery of the injuries suggested violence for violence's sake; the work of a sick and sadistic mind.

The killer had pounced on Rachel, police believed, after watching her progress across the common from a small, raised hillock adjoining Windmill Wood. From his vantage point, he would have been able to see Rachel and her little boy as they meandered slowly across a piece of open land and then wound their way down into the shady copse, young Alex and the scampering dog, Molly, having fun in the sun. From his perch the killer would also have the advantage of a visual scan of the area to tell him that no-one else was in the vicinity to be able to witness, or prevent, the dreadful deed he was about to perpetrate. He could see that the coast was clear for murder and that his victim was walking into his trap.

He slipped down a steep, but little-used, path at the side of the hillock, made from the spoil of the A3 London to Guildford road when it was built years before. Suddenly, he was there, in front of Rachel, menacing her with a razor-edged sheath knife. Two sharp prods to her chest drew blood and, in seconds, turned her idyllic stroll on the common into sheer terror. She was goaded at knife point, away from the footpath and into the protective shelter of a cluster of trees some ten yards away. Alex was cast aside with a dismissive blow to the face. Seconds later, Rachel's throat was slit from ear to ear, severing the larynx and preventing her from screaming for help. The little boy's cries of despair faded in the morning air. The shock of the attack rendered Alex speechless and paralysed with fear. It explained why no-one on the common that morning — and there were more than 500 — heard any sound from the copse where the young mother met such a violent end.

Rachel was a fit five feet four inches tall and weighed eight and a half stone. She would have fought like a tiger to defend herself and her son, given half an opportunity, but the killer had given her no chance whatsoever. He had struck with such swiftness, such severity, that Rachel was powerless to resist.

It was clear to police that the maniac had lain in wait at the edge of the wood, ready to ambush Rachel as she wandered, oblivious to the lurking danger, on a walk she enjoyed three or four times a week with her little boy. The exact point where the killer launched the attack was marked by Alex's green T-shirt lying on the ground. Rachel had been carrying it in her hand after Alex complained of feeling too hot as he played with Molly. Rachel then dropped the T-shirt in abject fear as the killer confronted her. Close by were shoeprints matching the pair that Rachel was wearing. This was the exact spot, police were sure, where the nightmare began for Rachel and her little boy.

However, was this a purely random killing — a pretty girl in the wrong place at the wrong time — or was Rachel a specific target? Perhaps she had once smiled innocently at a man on the common and the signals had been disastrously misinterpreted.

Home Office pathologist Dr Richard Shepherd — one of the country's most experienced investigators of murder, suspicious death and suicide — estimated that the attack on Rachel took three minutes from beginning to end. Even after she was dead, the sadistic assault on her body continued, the knife being driven into her body with such ferocity that an outline of the hilt was imprinted on her flesh. Whatever foul sex act the killer had perpetrated was carried out literally at the point of death or just after. Dr Shepherd was of the opinion that Rachel had either been subjected to anal rape — buggered — or had been violated with the handle of a knife or some similar implement. Bruising on little

Alex's cheek suggested that he had probably been struck a glancing blow by the killer sometime during the attack which he had so tragically been forced to witness. Perhaps, the police wondered, Alex had been threatened first in order to make his frightened mother comply with the killer's wishes. Had he, perhaps, tried against impossible odds, to help her in her desperate plight? It was all conjecture at that stage. What would the boy remember after such a harrowing ordeal? Would he, perhaps, eventually be the key to finding the man who had so brutally murdered his mother? How would they unlock his mind?

Within hours of the murder, Alex was in the tender care of experts whose twofold task was to minimise the emotional damage he must have suffered and, they hoped, elicit from him any tiny morsel of information which might assist the police in identifying the killer. So shocked was the little boy that he formed an instant bond with the policewoman who nursed him carefully while awaiting the arrival of an ambulance. He had found brief sanctuary amid the horror. He gripped the policewoman tightly, just as he had held on to his mummy earlier, refusing to let go. The WPC decided to go with him to hospital, cuddling him affectionately, her uniform soiled by the blood and mud covering his tiny body. That was the picture of little Alex which became indelibly printed on Mike Wickerson's memory, an image he will remember forever. 'The little boy was totally silent, just staring into space,' said the detective, himself the father of three children. 'It was at that very moment the full horror of what had happened dawned on me. It was simply the worst experience in twenty-six years of police work and something that will be with me to my dying day.'

As Alex was being taken to the safety of the hospital, the police were faced with breaking the news of the murder to his father, grandparents and other members of the family — one of the most unenviable tasks in the police service. Rachel had been provisionally identified through the registration number of her silver Volvo estate car which she had left in the Windmill car park before she set off on her walk with Alex and Molly. Police traced her boyfriend, Andre Hanscombe, at his job as a motorcycle courier based in north-east London. Andre had stopped at a phone box to make a call home just to see how Rachel and Alex were and to say 'I love you'. A policeman answered. Rachel was dead. Suddenly, out of the blue, Andre's life was shattered. As grief overpowered him he howled like an animal at the roadside. A former tennis coach, Andre then undertook the heartbreaking task of carrying out the mortuary identification of the pretty, vibrant blonde he had met and fallen in love with three years earlier at a swimming pool where she was the holiday lifeguard. Now she lay cold and lifeless on a mortuary slab. It seemed incomprehensible. Only hours earlier he had kissed her goodbye, had playfully tapped young Alex on the knuckles as he hung over the banisters, laughing. The bitter irony of her death on Wimbledon Common, he told detectives, was that she had chosen to go there for her walks with Alex because she felt safer than in the parks nearer their home in Clapham, south London.

Finding Rachel's parents, former army officer Andrew Nickell and his wife Monica, proved more of a problem. They were away from their smart modern home in Ampthill, Bedfordshire, on an extended holiday in the USA and Canada. Neither Andre, nor Rachel's brother Mark, then 25, knew precisely where they were staying, only a telephone number in case of emergencies. The police knew that the moment Rachel's murder was headline news, reporters from British newspapers would be jetting to Canada to track down the Nickells for interviews and background stories. The thought that Mr and Mrs Nickell could hear such heartbreaking news from jetlagged journalists appalled John Bassett and the murder team. They urged the Canadian police to pull out all the stops to make contact with the Nickells before the British press found them.

It took four days to trace the couple to their Great Lakes holiday home at Bridgenorth, Ontario, where they were staying with Andrew's sister Shirley Knowles and her husband John. The Nickells returned from a day's sightseeing over the border in the USA, to find a note pinned to the door asking them to call the local police station in connection with a 'serious family problem'. There they were told that there had been a death in the family and that Mr Nickell should wait and talk to his son for a fuller explanation. However, Mr Nickell insisted on being told, there and then, what had happened. More than 3,000 miles from home, Andrew and Monica Nickell learned that their beloved daughter was dead, but they were given only the briefest of details by the Canadian police. It was shock enough. They were left agonising . . . why, where, how?

Their son Mark, a merchant banker working in the City of London, had caught a flight from Gatwick airport to be with them in their hour of need and he arrived in Canada soon afterwards, accompanied by two detectives from Wimbledon, to tell his distraught folks the painful details of Rachel's murder. The family sat and grieved into the night, enduring together the dreadful pain of such a tragic loss, angry at the injustice of it all, wondering what kind of man could have taken such a precious life. They flew back to England together on the earliest available flight, with the murder team's Detective Constable Paul Miller and trainee investigator Mark Murdoch, to find that the murder inquiry had grown into one of Scotland Yard's biggest and most emotionally charged investigations for years, amid ever-increasing public concern that no-one had yet been arrested and charged.

Andrew and Monica Nickell's first thought was for their grandson. They found him in the care of a leading child psychologist, comforted by daddy Andre, always at hand, and surrounded by toys, sent in by wellwishers from all over the country, for Alex's plight had touched the nation's heart.

A fingertip search at the murder scene had failed to yield any sign of a murder weapon or any other significant evidence. To the dismay of the police, the forensic experts — the laboratory 'detectives' who are so vital in the modern-day battle against crime — had been unable to discover any biological evidence, such as blood, semen, hair, skin tissue or saliva, which could be from the killer, either on Rachel's body or at the scene of the crime. Without such vital samples there would be no chance of scientists producing a DNA 'genetic fingerprint' to help to trap the killer. With the range of sophisticated detection aids that are available to the police in modern crime detection, it was unusual for there to be no forensic evidence or fingerprints whatsoever. Was the killer just lucky or was he cunning enough to have deliberately ensured that he left no clues behind? There were various footprints around the murder scene, apart from Rachel's, but many people walked in those woods. None the less, casts were made of every tread in the hope that, one day, they would match those of the murderer's shoes.

The last person to see Rachel alive was actor Roger McKern as he cycled across the common on his way to rehearsals of A Midsummer Night's Dream at the Wimbledon Theatre. He was able to pinpoint the time and place exactly. He had stopped on his old boneshaker bike to check the time, fearing that he was running late and deciding which route would be quickest for him to take. It was exactly 10:20 a.m. He knew he could do it in ten minutes on the hard track leading off the common so he switched from the gravel track which was clogging his tyres. The pretty blonde and her little boy, walking at almost a dawdle on a grassy open area between the car park and Windmill Wood, caught his eye. He thought no more about it as he arrived on time at the theatre. That evening he heard the dreadful details of Rachel's murder on the news. He telephoned Wimbledon police and asked if the little boy involved was of mixed race. Yes, said detectives who knew that they now had an important sighting of Rachel when she was just minutes from her encounter with evil.

From the mass of interviews conducted by police on and around the common, it was clear that no-one had actually seen the killer attack Rachel — apart from her own son — or had observed a bloodsoaked man running from the area. The best early leads were the sighting of a short-haired man stooping to wash his hands in a ditch close to the murder scene and a man with a pony tail spotted hurriedly leaving the common shortly after the body was discovered. Neither gave the police a positive line of inquiry but, amid the unprecedented deluge of information that was flooding into the incident room for processing and computer analysis, detectives were hopeful that a 'fancied' suspect would be quickly identified. From the start, they believed it would be someone living locally, for one fact emerged very rapidly in the inquiry — if Wimbledon Common was a haven for innocent walkers, keep-fit fanatics and family fun days, it was also a magnet for every type of sex pest known to mankind. Report after report came in of flashers, gay sex, group sex, paedophiles spying on kiddies, odd happenings in the dead of night . . . a veritable directory of unnatural behaviour.

When a criminal records check was run on known sex offenders who might be suspects for Rachel's murder, it threw up the quite astonishing fact that over one hundred convicted perverts and sex attackers lived within a mile or two of the common. If difficult to start with, the task of the police was beginning to look daunting.

Every scrap of information, from whatever source, was fed into the police state-of-the-art crimefighting computer called HOLMES. It may seem to allude to the great Baker Street detective but, officially, it is termed the Home Office Large Major Enquiry System. The public abhorrence at Rachel's murder had produced such a tremendous response from the public, anxious that the killer should be caged as quickly as possible, that the detective force was increased to 54 to check out every possible lead. Costs soared, overtime bills mounted, sixteen-hour days became the norm for squad detectives, with every man and woman on the team sharing a solid determination that one day they would catch the monster who had killed Rachel Nickell. They had the technology, they had the commitment, all they needed was that little bit of luck so vital in every police investigation.

There were many 'hot' leads which, frustratingly, withered and died. Momentarily, a man in a red sweater emerged as a possible candidate for investigation. He was spotted by several witnesses who had been in the vicinity of the common on the day of the murder. The HOLMES computer (which, if it had been used in the Yorkshire Ripper inquiry would have pinpointed Peter Sutcliffe after five murders instead of thirteen) was becoming agitated. Suddenly, the police had sightings of the sweater-clad man in a dozen different locations. Could this be a fleeing suspect, making his way from the common? The explanation soon became clear. A golf tournament was being played on the common's old-established links course on the morning of the murder and one of the longstanding obligations of players was to wear a red sweater so that they would be easily identifiable and to give unsuspecting members of the public an opportunity to keep clear of any dangerously hit golf balls. The 'man in red' reported by so many people was, in fact, a number of the identically dressed golfers spotted at a variety of different locations. It was just one of many early false alarms.

Many of the players involved in the charity golf contest, organised by supermarket giant Tesco, had been teeing off close to the Windmill area as Rachel began her fateful stroll into the woods. None heard or saw anything of the awful tragedy so close at hand. The police asked all 160 players to abandon the game temporarily and assemble in the clubhouse to assist in identifying the murder victim's car. They each moved to the Windmill car park to stand by their own vehicle. Each car was claimed, until there was just a silver Volvo left unattended in the corner. It was Rachel's. A registration check matched the name and address on documents found on her body.

The golfers' brightly striped marquee, erected just a few hundred yards from the murder scene, provided an almost carnival backdrop to the hectic police activity across the common. A mobile incident room was fitted with hot-line phones, there were scores of officers tracing potential witnesses, tracker dogs scouring the woods, scrubland and grass, divers searching the ponds and the police helicopter India 99 roaring overhead. As word filtered among the 160 players of the sheer brutality of the murder, the organisers of the golf tournament considered calling it off as a mark of respect. However, in the end they decided to carry on, but conversation was muted as the golfers sat down for their meal in the marquee. Par fours and birdies took a back seat to talk of the murder of the pretty girl out walking with her baby son just a few hundred yards away.

At 12:30 p.m. on the day of the murder, PC

Andrew Couch was on duty at the perimeter of the common near Putney Cemetery where an underpass leads to the Alton Estate in nearby Roehampton. His job was to keep the common sealed; to let no-one on or off without good reason. Some time in the next 30 minutes — he couldn't be precise about the time — he stopped a young man near the cemetery gates as he headed towards the common with a brown mongrel dog walking obediently at heel. PC Couch told him that the common was out of bounds because of a serious incident earlier in the day. In a brief exchange of conversation, the man told the officer he had been on the common with his dog between 8:15 and 8:50 that morning, that they had walked by the Curling Pond then back to the Alton Estate via the A3 underpass. He had seen nothing suspicious on his travels, he said. His casual demeanour gave the officer no cause for concern but, for the record, the officer jotted his name and address in his notebook before the man, in T-shirt and jeans, turned on his heel and strolled back towards his home in Ibsley Gardens, a few minutes' walk away. The man was Colin Francis Stagg, aged 29, unmarried and out of work, a resident of the Alton Estate for most of his life, a man who knew the common like his own back yard.

Five days after the murder inquiry was launched, a new senior officer joined the team — Detective Inspector Keith Pedder, drafted in from busy Brixton police station. He was a shrewd, straight-talking copper, highly rated in the job and earmarked for bigger things. Over the next two years and two months, Colin Stagg and Keith Pedder were to become inextricably linked in an extraordinary battle of minds as the police operation aimed at finding Rachel's killer became one of Scotland Yard's most expensive, challenging and ultimately frustrating cases in criminal history.

The Girl with Everything

When the time came to face the media, the dignity shown by Andrew Nickell must have taken up every last ounce of his innermost strength. He knew that, by appearing at a Scotland Yard press conference, he might somehow help the daughter he had lost; that a public appeal for assistance, any kind of help, might just provide the vital lead to Rachel's killer. It was something he had to do for Rachel. Theirs had been a very special relationship.

Until that dreadful day on Wimbledon Common, life had been good to the Nickells. Rachel was born on

23 November 1968, gifted with good looks, personality and brains. The bond with her father was strong, remaining solid even when she announced that she was pregnant with Alexander and intended to abandon her university education to become a full-time mother and bring him up. Mr and Mrs Nickell were delighted when Rachel moved into Andre's two-bedroom, second-floor flat in a Victorian house in Elmfield Road, Balham. The Nickells settled down, in happy anticipation of the joys of becoming grandparents, unembittered by the fact that many of their dreams for Rachel's future — of ambitions unfulfilled — had been forsaken. Rachel was happy and that was all that really mattered.

Less than three years later, the fact that Andrew Nickell could be facing a battery of cameras and reporters' questions at a Scotland Yard press conference seemed incomprehensible. Yet here he was, just five days after the savage murder of the daughter he adored, baring his soul in the hope that he could help to catch the perpetrator of such evil. He showed remarkable composure as he sat, with Mark close by, asking for help from the public in catching the monster who had robbed him of his daughter.

'Please don't let it happen again,' he begged. 'Next time it could be someone else's daughter, or mother, or wife.' Rachel, he said, was 'a shining light, a bright star in my life and everyone else's who knew her. Her happiness with Andre was so real you could almost touch it. She can never be replaced in our lives and we can only hope to pick up the pieces. But our lives will always be less rich now that she has gone.'

It was the poignant testimony of a caring father,

remembering the happiness his daughter had given and aware of the empty days that were now to come. There were so many proud memories for Andrew and Monica. They had raised their golden-haired daughter in an atmosphere of secure, middle-class respectability in the Essex village of Great Totham, near Colchester. Life always seemed so safe for the young Rachel. Their home in Beacon Wood epitomised solid good taste, large without being ostentatious, with neatly manicured lawns and roses round the door. Andrew had served for many years as an army officer and still walked with upright, military bearing. He now made a comfortable living as a shoe importer, permitting his family a life without financial worry. According to friend and former neighbour Marjorie Wells, the Nickells were 'the perfect family'. It could have sounded like a patronising cliché in the circumstances, if it hadn't been said with a simple sincerity that was echoed over and over again in that tiny community.

Rachel was a popular pupil at Great Totham Primary School and then won a place at Colchester High School for Girls, a selective grammar school, by gaining a series of high marks in her eleven plus. Her talents were evident in and out of the classroom. She was such a natural at dancing that she could have shone on the West End stage. She also showed enormous kindness, both to animals and to her fellow human beings. She organised Christmas parties for old folk and for disabled children. She acted in school plays and sang in the choir. Before she was sixteen, her striking good looks brought offers of modelling work but, sensibly, she turned them down to concentrate on her school books. In the five years she spent at Colchester High, she left headmistress Dr Aline Black in no doubt that great times beckoned in the years to come. Dr Black described Rachel as 'a lovely and active young woman who had great potential and a wonderful future ahead of her'. Rachel left Colchester High with nine O-Levels, including the sciences, English, art, French and history, winning four A-grades and five B-grades. Dr Black's grief that so much had been lost was clearly visible as news of the murder was broken to her and to fellow teachers who had helped to mould the young Rachel Nickell.

Outside school hours Rachel had been equally active. She was a star pupil with the Essex Dance Theatre in Chelmsford and principal Debbie Holme had had visions of a showbusiness career for her. 'She could easily have made it into the chorus lines in West End shows,' she said. 'She had the ability and the looks. She passed all her exams with ease. It is so tragic to think so much has gone to waste.'

Rachel's mother — as dark as her daughter was blonde — became a swimming coach at nearby Witham Dolphins Club in order to encourage her children to enjoy the water. Again Rachel excelled, becoming a particularly stylish diver. Before Rachel died, she, too, had begun passing on her skills to Alex at regular mother and toddler swimming sessions at the Balham Leisure Centre, close to their flat. She was anxious that Alex should feel safe in the water and enjoy swimming just as much as she had done as a child.

Writer Frances Hubbard spent days researching the life and times of Rachel Nickell, talking to people who had known her. She came to this conclusion in an article in the *Daily Express*:

'In its own way the whole country has been jolted by Rachel's murder. She stood for qualities of honesty and goodness that are supposed to triumph over dark and violent forces. This week, on a lonely stretch of Wimbledon Common, evil won.' It reflected so well the sentiments of all involved in the case.

At Wimbledon police station John Bassett and his detectives studied the album of colour photographs taken of Rachel's body straight after the murder, and knew all about evil. Each testimony the detectives read, to the caring lifestyle of the young mother whose death now occupied them round the clock, reinforced their determination to hunt down the man who had taken so much away. It is easy for policemen's emotions to become anaesthetised, dealing as frequently as they do with man's inhumanities to man, woman and child. Not on this squad. These were husbands and fathers as well as detectives. They knew about loving families and the damage that had been done.

As the police carefully searched Rachel's home, a necessary formality in such circumstances, they had yet another insight into the kind of devotion she had shown her son. They found a book called *I'll Always Love You*, the story of a small boy learning to cope with the grief of losing his pet dog. It was the last bedtime story Rachel ever read to Alex and his first real lesson in growing up. She had borrowed the book from the local library and read it to Alex as they cuddled on the bed the night before she died. In it, a small boy cries for 'the best dog in the world'. Each night he told his pet, 'I will always love you.' Rachel wanted to teach her son gently about the hurts of life; to show him there are tears as well as laughter. She had chosen the book, along with three others, to top up Alex's stock of bedtime stories. The librarian who served her remembered the moment well. 'When she came in I was feeling a bit down and she told me to cheer up,' she said. 'She was that sort of person, so cheerful. She was such a caring and committed mum who obviously enjoyed every minute of bringing up her son. She read regularly to him. It was something she felt was very important.'

The book Rachel read to Alex that night ended with the little boy and his family burying their pet dog and sobbing at his graveside. 'We buried Elfie together,' said the text. 'We all cried and hugged each other.'

The very next day little Alex was to face the biggest hurt in his life, one which no amount of hugs and tears would ever fully mend.

Andre, olive-skinned and ruggedly handsome, had often talked with Rachel of moving from London to the fresh air of the countryside or even to France, somewhere near the sea. They tentatively approached estate agents about putting their flat on the market for £85,000. They'd had a 'bite' at £80,000 and excitement surged about the possibilities ahead. 'They had so many hopes and working as a leather-clad motorbike courier was purely a temporary measure to pay the mortgage while he pursued his ambition of becoming a tennis professional. He had played semi-professionally and had coached at the Roger Taylor tennis school in Portugal. Rachel had undertaken a few modelling assignments (she was often likened to the stunning blonde in the television Timotei shampoo ad) and had been offered a contract with an agency whose other models included Robert de Niro's stepdaughter. She also nurtured a hope that, maybe, when Alex was a little older, she could break into television and get a job as a presenter like Ulrika Jonsson, to whom she also bore more than a passing resemblance. For the time being, however, she had selflessly put motherhood before her own personal ambitions.

Rachel had met and fallen in love with Andre in September 1988, when she was reading for an English degree and took a holiday job as a lifeguard at a swimming pool in Richmond, Surrey. At roughly the same time, her parents decided to leave Great Totham and move to a pleasant modern house in The Avenue, Ampthill in Bedfordshire. Rachel, Andre and little Alex were regular and welcome visitors to the house. Rachel was just stunning, said neighbour Sue Burridge as she recalled how young Alex had been taken to the annual street party the year before and had thoroughly enjoyed it. 'Such a lovely family, always doing things together.'

And it was as a family that they grieved and began the delicate job of helping Alex back to normality — if, indeed, normality would ever be possible. Every step was a constant reminder of their lost daughter. One day Alex innocently picked up a pair of Rachel's earrings, given to her by her mother as a twenty-first-birthday present, and asked, 'Will Mummy mind if I wear them?'

Mrs Nickell replied, 'Well, Mummy doesn't want them any more.'

Said Andrew Nickell, 'That was the way it had to be. It is very important that we talk about Rachel.'

Rachel drove from Balham to her parents' Ampthill

home at least once a week to visit with Alex. Mr and Mrs Nickell adored the curly-haired little boy. Rachel's father now regrets bitterly — though unreasonably — that he and Monica ever went on their Canadian holiday of a lifetime. 'If we had been at home Rachel might have been spending the day with us, not visiting Wimbledon Common,' he said, just wishing he could turn back the clock.

Less than a month after the murder, the family celebrated Alex's third birthday — just a small affair with Andre, the grandparents and a couple of family friends. They gave Alex a bicycle and a helmet to wear when he rode it.

The aching gap in the family's life seemed like a chasm as they wondered daily who could have done such a thing to such a sweet-natured girl and left so much grief behind. They also wondered whether the police would ever catch him. 'He's out there but he's faceless,' said Andrew. 'I think he is a complete lunatic, a psychopath, to do what he did to Rachel. You just hope it's right when the pathologist tells you she died quickly. It is very difficult to focus anger or revenge on someone you can't picture. When he is standing in front of me and I know for certain it is the person who has taken my daughter, then that is when it will be hard. All of us know that the worst is yet to come.

If the profile of the killer gradually emerging at the Wimbledon incident room was to be believed, Mr Nickell's fears were well founded.

A few days after the murder, Andre, though clearly shattered by grief, made the bold decision to take Alex back to Wimbledon Common. He wanted to show him that it wasn't the trees or the grass or the ponds that were bad. He didn't want the boy growing up frightened of his own shadow. Child psychiatrists recommended a gentle visit to the common where bouquets of flowers and messages of sympathy lay near the spot where Rachel died. It was, they said, part of the healing process that might one day help Alex to obliterate the horror once and for all from his mind.

Newsmen accompanied Andre, Alex and the police. Both Andre and Andrew Nickell made impassioned pleas to the media that the little boy's face should not be plastered across the next day's newspapers or on television screens. Uppermost in Andre's mind at that time was the fact that because Alex was the only witness to his mother's murder and the killer was still free, the boy's life could be in very real danger — silence the boy and the only person who could identify the murderer would be safely out of the way forever. It was a chilling thought. Only one paper ignored the family request that Alex's photo be disguised — *The Sun*. The following day they showed Alex full face, walking with his father on the common. Every other paper had carefully blanked out the little boy's features. The family and police were outraged at *The Sun*'s behaviour. Within hours, the Press Complaints Commission was deluged with protests in what was to signal the start of a long and prickly relationship between the press and the police throughout the Rachel Nickell investigation.

Andre's return to the common evoked memories of the advice he had given Rachel a couple of years earlier after she had complained of being constantly propositioned by sex pests in other parks. She had exercised nearer home in Tooting and Clapham but had become upset at the unwanted attention her striking good looks involuntarily encouraged. She complained to Andre and her parents. They advised her that Wimbledon Common would be a better bet, as it was a better-class area, with permanent ranger patrols out on horseback and always plenty of people about to help in the event of danger. Rachel tried it and became entranced with the common's woodland walks, gently undulating hills, streams, the ponds — Queensmere, Kingsmere, Curling and Stag — and, most of all, by the huge windmill made famous by Baden Powell, founder of the Boy Scouts. Rain or shine, she drove there most days in her old but reliable W-reg Volvo, to give Alex the fresh air and exercise she felt he needed. Even the attentions of a perverted 'flasher' exposing himself to her on one occasion did not deter her regular visits. Police did not believe the incident was connected with her murder. It was, unfortunately, a regular hazard endured by many women on the common. Actress Jenny Seagrove then the pretty girlfriend of film director and law and order campaigner Michael Winner, fled from two suspicious men just days before Rachel was attacked. Like Rachel, she was walking her dog, a spaniel called Tasha, across the common when the incident happened. Although uninjured, she vowed not to go back to the common until the killer was caught.

A specially planted young tree is now growing close to the spot where Rachel died to provide a natural, simple shrine to her memory for many years to come. A wooden seat, dedicated to her memory, serves as a more practical reminder of a life so cruelly lost.

Five days after the murder, the *News of the World* offered a reward of £15,000 for information leading to the arrest and conviction of the killer. Police hoped fervently that this might persuade some mother, wife or girlfriend to call with that vital scrap of information so desperately needed to catch the man who had killed an angel and wrecked a family. The calls flooded in. More names, more addresses, more leads were chased but the trail stayed ominously cold.

By now, ten days after the murder, Alex was starting to chatter again, as if the nightmare was slowly fading. Would this be the time gently to coax from his mind any details that could lead to identifying the killer? Andre was just grateful that his son's courage was winning through. 'Alex is doing all right,' he said. 'Kids are incredibly strong. I was told he would cope with this better than me. I didn't believe it then but I believe it now. He has an incredible will to live, really wants to go on.' He said Alex had accepted 'more than anyone' the fact of his mother's death. 'Kids put on an incredible acting performance to protect us, to protect me,' he said. 'He only lets his guard down maybe once or twice a day. I'm trying to keep the door open before he closes it and buries it forever. He may be young but he knows what happened.'

Andre was overwhelmed at the enormous kindness shown by so many people but resigned to the long, bleak road ahead without Rachel at his side. 'The only thing I have left is to try to heal the wounds inflicted on my son. All the messages have given me the courage to consider the possibility that there may be a life somewhere left for Alex that is worth living.'

Andre had experienced sadness enough himself as a boy when his parents' marriage had ended in acrimony and divorce. From the age of ten, he lived with his Zimbabwe-born father until he was old enough to fend for himself. Apparently, his father was an authoritarian schoolmaster whom Andre grew to hate. He prayed that there would never be such bitterness between himself and Alex. That seemed unimaginable as father and son grew closer by the day, each helping to heal the other's emotional wounds in his own way. The detectives on the case, both male and female, had become entranced with young Alex. His good looks, enormous expressive eyes and bright, intelligent personality won the hearts of officers like Bassett, Wickerson and Pedder, family men whose careers to date had seen service in some of the toughest areas of police work. Alex Hanscombe became someone very special to the team trying to find the maniac who had murdered his mother.

A woman doctor trained in child psychology was tentatively testing the water to see if Alex was ready to talk about the day his mummy died. She was planning to use play sessions with dolls and toys with different colour hair and different skin complexions, to try to extract a description of the killer. John Basset was optimistic. 'He is talking and it is very encouraging,' he said. 'He has a good vocabulary. His verbal skills are very good because his mum and dad read to him regularly and talked to him a lot. It would be marvellous if he could turn round and give me a brilliant description, a photofit. I'm hopeful but, on the other hand, I don't want to place too much hope because it can easily be dashed.'

At the murder scene floral tributes still lay at the

foot of an oak tree close to where Rachel died. Attached to a posy, one note read, 'Hope they find the animal that did this to you and your son. God bless you and your child.'

On 22 July, still seeking that elusive piece of information which would help them to find that animal, police tried a memory-jogging exercise. A friend of Rachel's, called Jane, offered to help in a reconstruction of Rachel's last walk in the hope that it would spark the recollections of anyone who was in the area at the time of the killing and who might have a piece of information stored away which could help to solve the jigsaw. Courageous Jane, slim and strikingly pretty like Rachel, was clearly overcome by the experience as she retraced Rachel's footsteps, a little boy called Luke playing the role of Alex and her own dog, Ralph, trotting behind like Molly had. After the reconstruction was over and the cameramen had moved away, she wandered off towards Windmill Wood for a private moment alone, possibly for a personal farewell to her friend. It was, she said, the last time she would ever visit the common until the killer was safely behind bars. Another of the bouquets lying at the murder scene echoed the sentiment. Signed 'Kathy, Andy and Major the dog', it read 'May it not be too long before the beastly character is caught and brought to justice so that everyone may enjoy the peace and tranquility again.'

John Bassett, who had not long to go now in his career, certainly hoped it wouldn't be too long. He said, 'The man who did this has got to be mentally and emotionally distressed. He may be sitting at home now, reading newspaper accounts or watching television. If he has one shred of common decency in him he will give himself up. The ferocity of the attack was such that this man has to be abnormal. It must be preying on his conscience. I appeal to the man who committed this heinous crime to give himself up.'

It was a forlorn hope. Any man who could murder and mutilate a young mother in front of her son clearly had no conscience. Of course he was abnormal, but just how terrifyingly abnormal was to be illustrated when John Bassett decided to call in the experts in abnormality, the psychologists who deal daily with the sickest minds in our society. It was to be one of the greatest challenges yet to a developing technique in modern-day crimefighting.

At a moving ceremony near her parents' home in Ampthill Rachel was buried on 3 August. Brave Alex, the last of the family to see her alive, clutched a heart-shaped balloon as he said his final goodbye. He gripped the helium-filled balloon, which had a Thomas the Tank Engine motif on it, throughout the 30-minute service at picturesque, twelfth-century St Andrew's Church, bedecked with flowers in what Monica and Andrew Nickell wanted to be a celebration of their daughter's life, rather than a mourning for her death. Alex sat dry-eyed on his weeping father's lap, detectives flanking them on each side. By now Detective Constable Miller and Detective Constable Nick Sparshatt had become the constant companions of Andre and his little boy, both for security reasons and for their vital moral support in the face of such grief. More than bodyguards, they had become firm friends. In particular, the police stayed close by young Alex in case his memory was suddenly jogged and he uttered a phrase, a name, a description, which might help to solve his mother's murder. Sporting a jaunty baseball cap, Alex was carried by his grieving father from the church to a waiting car for the five-minute journey to Bedford Crematorium. With him went a pretty posy of peach carnations bearing the poignant message:

'Mummy, you gave me all your being, every moment of your time and always all your love.' As he was due to read an ancient American Indian burial prayer to the 160 mourners, close family and friends, Andre could not control his tears. The emotional service became too much for him and Andrew Nickell stepped in to read the moving words instead:

> 'Do not stand at my grave and weep.
> I am not there, I do not sleep.
> I am a thousand winds that blow.
> I am the diamond glints on snow.
> I am the sunlight on ripened grain.
> I am the gentle autumn rain.
> When you awaken in the morning hush,
> I am the uplifting rush of quiet birds in
> circled flight.
> I am the soft stars that shine at night.
> Do not stand at my grave and cry.
> I am not there, I did not die.'

The poem and its message perfectly symbolised the love Andre had shared with Rachel. It was, her father recalled, an instant attraction which had developed into a deep and lasting love. On the day of their first meeting

Rachel had called her mother to tell her, 'Mummy, I have just met the man I want to spend the rest of my life with. I just know.'

Andrew Nickell said, 'Her sparkling phone calls nearly every day told us of her joy in Andre and Alex. Rachel was straight, bright and shining. She radiated love, good humour, warmth and generosity wherever she went.' His voice faltering as he choked back his tears, he added, 'She had an unconscious capacity to bring out the best in the people she met. She was an adoring and conscientious mother. I believe the good that people do lives after them, bringing out the best in those they leave behind.'

The mood of the funeral was reflected in the opening words of the service given by Ampthill rural dean, the Reverend David Lewthwaite: 'Violence shall not have the last word.' Not in that family, so close in their great loss, it wouldn't, that was certain. Rachel's memory was bright on the service sheets. Printed on them, as a poignant reminder for each of the mourners, was a sketch of pink flowers bordering a message Rachel had sent to a friend on a Christmas card a few years earlier. In bright fuchsia pink, in her own handwriting, it said 'Lots and lots of Love, Rachel' and was sealed with two kisses. A treasured memory indeed. It was a deeply moving farewell to a girl who clearly had been someone very special to very many people.

The previous day, one thousand men, women and children, some of them on horseback, some who had never known Rachel, had marched in silent tribute to her on Wimbledon Common itself. The procession, with many women weeping quietly at the memory of her death, set off from Wimbledon Village to walk slowly to the spot where the killer had struck her down. Wreaths with touching messages were scattered on the ground. Family friend Gordon Hammond addressed the crowd, who had come from all walks of life, in all kinds of clothes, with a message from Andre Hanscombe saying how surprised and moved he was by their mass display of sympathy. He said his heart also went out to other murder victims. 'Man's savagery and brutality is inflicting this kind of pain and suffering in the world every single moment of the day and night. If you shed a tear for Rachel, she would also have you shed one for every victim of violence.' They all knew Rachel Nickell a little bit better as they stood in solemn reflection.

Rachel's ashes were interred in a cliff-top churchyard on the south coast, beside her grandmother's, a few days after the funeral, with just close family there to say a final farewell. It was there that Monica Nickell revealed just how close to total despair and suicide Andre Hanscombe had been after the murder. It was only his love for Alex which had pulled him back from the brink. It had been so much worse for Andre, she said, because there had been no-one with him to share his grief. Despite her own family's efforts, Andre had borne most of the heartache on his own. 'It is better for Andrew and me because we have each other. It was far worse for Andre,' she said. 'Andrew feels dreadfully sad at losing Rachel, but it is me banging my head and screaming, "Why? Why? Why?" I have been going to church from time to time and I think I shall probably go a bit more now. It's very hard to imagine the mind of the person who did this. I cannot even think of putting a face to the killer. I don't think any of us can.' Alex had seen his mother's body and accepted that she had gone forever. 'He has seen the ashes and knows exactly what went on at the interrment,' said Mrs Nickell. 'We have told him the truth because it is not right to lie. We have got to help little Alex out as much as we possibly can.' Rachel, she said, had been with her grandmother when she died. 'She was always the favourite granddaughter,' she said. The family was coming to terms with its grief.

At murder headquarters the police were facing an unimaginable new dimension in death.

Uncontrollable Frenzy

Two of the world's leading experts in sex murders provided the Scotland Yard team with a frightening insight into the mind of Rachel Nickell's killer. Robert Ressler, a former FBI agent from America, and Paul Britton, a clinical psychologist from Leicester, worked separately but arrived at an uncannily similar conclusion. The murderer, they said, was a fantasy-crazed local man, a loner, white, in his mid-twenties and sexually inadequate. He was, they predicted, a man obsessed with violence and programmed to kill again.

Ressler, who originally coined the phrase 'serial killer', had spent a lifetime in hunting mass murderers and then interviewing them to find out what made them tick. He pioneered the technique of 'offender profiling' in America and used it to arrest more dangerous and disturbed sex killers than any man in the FBI's history. The secret of his success, he said, was getting right inside the minds of twisted killers, to discover why they commit such unspeakable horrors. To do this he interrogated some of America's most notorious criminals, including cult leader Charles Manson, sex monster Ted Bundy, who killed over 50 women, and John Wayne Gacy, who murdered 23 men and buried them under his house. His last interview was with Jeffrey Dahmer, the Milwaukee monster who butchered fifteen young men and ate parts of them for supper.

Ressler joined the FBI in 1970 and was instrumental in setting up the profiling centre at its Behavioral Science Unit which specialised in catching serial killers and the most extreme kind of sex offender. Now retired, he and his wife Betty still live close to the FBI training centre at Quantico, Virginia, which became famous to millions of cinemagoers when it was featured in *The Silence of the Lambs*. Ressler was flown to Britain by *The Sun* in the hope that his knowledge could help Scotland Yard to build up an accurate profile of Rachel's killer. It was strictly unofficial assistance but, in the absence of any serious leads, it might prove invaluable to the Wimbledon team. Ressler's track record proved a 90 per cent success rate. His evaluation of Rachel's killer was clearly worthy of police attention, despite initial reluctance by the Yard men to co-operate with an uninvited 'outsider', especially someone receiving a fee from a tabloid newspaper and with a recently published book on serial killers needing maximum publicity.

Paul Britton, on the other hand, was called in officially by the police in his capacity as Britain's leading authority on offender profiling. He, too, had devoted much of his life to delving into the darkest recesses of the criminal mind. His qualifications were impressive, his knowledge formidable. Slightly overweight and softly spoken, Britton exuded more of the air of a small-town bank manager than of a man whose case histories represented a catalogue of the most twisted and dangerous minds in Britain. He had seen the outer limits of sexual depravity many, many times.

Britton was respected the world over for the continued progress he was making in the field of offender profiling. His expertise had been used by the police in many parts of Britain for ten years and he was a member of the Association of Chief Police Officers' sub-committee on offender profiling. He also taught forensic psychology at Leicester and Sheffield Universities, a burgeoning discipline in a society which seems to produce an ever-increasing number of mind-warped offenders.

So, here were two formidable 'mind detectives' pitched against an elusive and devious adversary. It was clear to the police team within days of the murder that they were not going to be blessed with a lucky break in finding the killer and, in the absence of independent eye witnesses, fingerprints, forensic evidence or DNA samples, this inquiry was set to break new ground in the use of offender profiling as the basis for a future prosecution. When Detective Superintendent Bassett picked up the phone to call Paul Britton at the end of July he had no idea just how far down that road his team would be compelled to go or what repercussions would follow.

FBI sleuth Ressler was the first to produce his conclusions, after spending days examining the murder scene, scouring the high-rise blocks of the Alton Estate and eliciting what detailed information could be gleaned about the attack from available police sources and published reports. His profile, featured in *The Sun* on 1 August — sixteen days after the murder — was of a warped psycho in the mould of Norman Bates in the classic spinechiller *Psycho*. Ressler painted a portrait of a deeply disturbed, yet clever, loner who probably worshipped his mother, or her memory, and was sexually inadequate but fuelled by the most twisted of fantasies. Ressler documented his theories in a seven-page, 23-point report which was handed to Bassett's team and contained the chilling conclusion: 'He has got the taste of blood and could kill again.'

Ressler's profile suggested that the killer was a social misfit who kept to himself and was regarded by neighbours as a local loony, mistakenly believed to be harmless. Said Ressler: 'The degree of mutilation on Rachel leads me to believe the killer suffers some full-blown mental illness, possibly a split personality. His condition would make him act like an oddball, unable to make friends. He would be incapable of normal conversation and prone to outbursts of temper. He may swear at people in the street or do other strange things. He may come and go at odd times of the night as he more than likely suffers from insomnia.'

Rachel, said Ressler, was almost certainly his first victim. The killing bore the hallmarks of someone overcome by an unstoppable urge to strike out in an uncontrollable frenzy. And now that he had tasted death once he might not be satisfied and might be driven to kill again. He might already have filed the killing away in his mind as yet another fantasy and might not even realise he had done it.

Although weird, the killer was also intelligent, said Ressler. He would have had a chequered school history. He was probably bright to start with at school but in his teenage years he either dropped out completely or left early with few qualifications. The onset of mental disorder suffered by such a killer often begins at around fourteen or fifteen years old, said Ressler. It mainly affected people of high intelligence, rendering them incapable of concentration or discipline.

He would be sexually inadequate, frustrated, and had probably never had a proper relationship with a woman. His mental state rendered him incapable of a normal, caring, adult relationship. He had twisted fantasies about sex but could never approach a woman conventionally. He would be white and in his mid-twenties. His mental illness, which would normally take ten to fifteen years to develop, would have begun at puberty, then festered and grown over the next decade. From police clues, the ethnic mix of the area, crime statistics and the choice of victim, it was almost certain that Rachel was killed by a member of the same race, a white male, said the ex-policeman, putting all his years of experience into the chilling portrait.

The killer, concluded Ressler, lived alone or with an elderly parent, most likely in a council house or low-rent property. He would be too unstable to live with any woman apart from a close elderly relative who was most probably kind to him. He would arouse less suspicion living on a council estate — like the high rises within ten minutes' walk of Wimbledon Common. Wrote Ressler: 'As I toured the council areas I got a definite impression that this was the kind of area our man would live in.'

His appearance was likely to be distinctive. He would be dishevelled, dirty, unshaven and undernourished. People with his kind of sickness cannot take care of themselves. He would not wash or eat properly, making him look thin and unkempt.

He was probably the victim of neglect or abuse as a child. This probably took the form of sexual or mental abuse, possibly both. He did not have a normal childhood and found it difficult to mix with other youngsters, including any brothers or sisters of his own. He might well come from a broken home and have had a very unhappy upbringing.

He was almost definitely a woman hater. This type of killer nearly always had a distorted view of women, formed during childhood. His mother might have neglected or ill-treated him, or perhaps his father had — thereby giving him a 'mother worship' complex. His own upbringing would have coloured his view of families and family life. Ressler added, 'This was brought home to me by the fact that he allowed Rachel's little boy Alex to live. Either he sympathised with the toddler — seeing himself as a victim of abuse — or recognised his own unhappy childhood.'

Any unhappiness in Alex's life was certainly never evident until the day the mother he adored was killed before his eyes.

Paul Britton studied the grim evidence of the police photographs taken of Rachel's body at the scene of the murder and at the mortuary at Kingston Hospital, read the pathologist's reports and was given access to the police files, packed with all known information to date, to help him to assess what kind of creature had stalked and slain Rachel Nickell. His findings were unequivocal. He was convinced beyond doubt that Rachel had been the victim of a man suffering from a sexually deviant personality disturbance, a man inflamed by fantasies of torturing and humiliating women. The fantasies, ever growing in intensity, would dominate his life, leading eventually to the overwhelming urge to kill. In his twisted mind, they would contain scenes of young women forced to submit to his perverted desires, of women used purely as sex objects, of knives used in sadistic assaults, of both anal and vaginal intercourse and abuse. The 'masturbatory fantasies', as Britton termed them, would involve the killer tying up women, having total power and control over them, and culminate in him violently and sadistically killing the victim.

It was Britton's firm opinion that, in the Rachel Nickell murder, there was classic evidence of a dangerous sexual deviant acting out his fantasies in real life. The killer had fulfilled his lust with the ultimate degree of horror. The victim, believed Britton, had been chosen because she fitted the sexual images in his fantasies: young, pretty, respectable, middle class, all that was unattainable to him. That she was sexually interfered with after death indicated that it was a murder for pure sexual gratification with no desire for any kind of emotional relationship. It did not involve Rachel's co-operation or consent. The attack would have caused great fear and distress in the victim, inflaming the killer's lust with a sense of power.

Britton used the phrase 'personality disturbance' carefully. It was not, he stressed, a disorder. That would imply some permanent or long-standing condition. This man's emotional turmoil was temporary, a loss of control for a relatively short period of time, after which he would revert back to apparent normality — until the next time.

Rachel, said Britton, had clearly been prodded with a knife to force her, trembling with fear, off the footpath and into the woods to the killer's preferred place of attack, away from the risk of being seen and apprehended. This, said Britton, would be consistent with the sense of power so important in the killer's fantasies. Rachel's body had been dragged, or rolled after death, under a silver birch where her jeans and underwear were removed and her buttocks exposed in a prominent position. The interference with her anus and vagina had lasted for a very short period of time and involved the deliberate and careful insertion of some kind of implement into the anal area. The killer, he said, would have been highly excited by Rachel's 'submissive acquiescence', but he had showed no 'functional interest' in little Alex.

The attack on Rachel's throat, said the psychologist, was far more vigorous than that needed to kill her and such extreme violence would be a recognisable theme in the killer's fantasies. Such powerful and deviant psycho sexuality would be found, said Britton, in only a minute proportion of sexual deviants in the British public. Probably only one in two or three million of all adult males could be suffering from this condition. In effect, among the entire population of Britain there could be no more than a dozen such dangerously deviant men — a frightening enough statistic for the police to contend with.

Britton also believed that the killer was likely to be a young man living nearby and a regular user of the common, having an intimate knowledge of all the escape routes which would have led him to safety after leaving Rachel for dead with the traumatised child cuddling her corpse.

Three weeks into the inquiry, the murder squad were faced with these deeply disturbing analyses of the unknown, unseen killer on the common — a lone wolf of a man with a burning cauldron of hate and lust in his mind, prepared at a whim to wipe out the life of a beautiful young woman in front of her son, for some transitory sexual gratification, and ready to inflict the same pain and suffering again when the urge took him. But who was he? Where was he? Would they find him in time?

It was solicitor's wife Jane Harriman who came up with the best lead to date. Like Rachel, she had been on the common on 15 July for a happy family outing. With her four youngsters, aged between three and thirteen in a boisterous mood, she set off at 9:45 a.m. from the Windmill car park, over towards Jerrys Hill in the general direction of the A3 which runs along the south-west boundary of the common. The family group strolled along a grassy path, then pushed through close-growing bushes to make their way into a small wood. Mrs Harriman spotted a man walking towards her and was instantly apprehensive. He was about five feet ten inches tall, with close-cropped dark brown hair, wearing a white T-shirt and dark trousers and clutching a dark-coloured sports bag. He was in his late twenties or early thirties, with a thin sort of baby face. It was just about 10:10 a.m. when they passed each other, going in opposite directions. Her youngest son, Fred, was taking an intense interest in some rabbit droppings as the man passed close by and Mrs Harriman's gaze wandered between his face and that of the little boy. She thought he might have heard young Fred's observations about the rabbit droppings and was ready to smile at him if he had, but he turned his head sharply as if to hide his features.

The man walked on about eight feet past Mrs Harriman, appeared to pause momentarily, then walked on again. The children continued playing nearby as she arrived at the Curling Pond and watched while her dog splashed with another in the water. The fun and games ended when the owner of the other dog, identified later as Pauline Fleming, left and headed towards the woods. Mrs Harriman sat on some nearby logs — remnants of the 1987 hurricane — to watch the world go by for a few minutes as her children played on the edge of the Curling Pond. Then the sinister stranger she had seen some six or seven minutes earlier appeared again. He walked round the other side of the pond and headed, ominously, in the direction the other woman had taken minutes earlier. He had an odd look on his face and walked with a slight but distinctive stoop. 'He was walking briskly, as if in a hurry, but a bit nervously,' Mrs Harriman told police. Her protective instincts aroused, she called the children because she was now feeling nervous about strange men in the woods behind her. After a few more minutes the stooping man emerged again from the woods on her left-hand side. This time he was heading back along the route he had taken earlier, towards the hillock next to Windmill Wood and its commanding views over the nearby terrain. She spotted what appeared to be a thin belt or strap round his waist, over his T-shirt. She was sure it hadn't been there earlier. She watched him disappear back through the gap in the trees and vanish from sight. By now, she was so suspicious that she decided to take a look in the wood to make sure no harm had come to the other woman. She found nothing amiss. Mrs Harriman and her children continued their stroll, perhaps fortunate that her brief but anxious search of the wood had been so cursory. Rachel Nickell was almost certainly already lying dead as they passed by little more than twenty yards away.

Had Jane Harriman brushed past the killer on that woodland track? Was he heading for the murder scene as she watched him lope by with his bag in his hand? It was about 10:23 a.m. when she had seen the stranger for the final time. Police already knew from Roger McKern that, at 10:20, Rachel and Alex were walking from the opposite direction towards the sheltering trees of Windmill Wood. Had the paths of the stooping man and Rachel Nickell crossed just minutes later with such disastrous consequences? Jane Harriman was anxious to help in any way she could and assisted police from

Scotland Yard's Facial Identification unit in building up an artist's impression of the sinister stroller in Windmill Wood. The final video-enhanced picture shown to her a few days later was, she said, 'a very good likeness'. It was to provide the police with the lead they so sorely needed. With detectives, Mrs Harriman went back to the common to retrace the exact route she had walked on the day of the murder. It was clear that she and her children must have been following the same route as Rachel and Alex, just minutes ahead of them, going at the same casual pace. The man with the bag had to be the number-one suspect. Armed with the videofit and the psychologists' frightening reports, the police were ready for a major publicity drive to find him.

Was it the same person, police wondered, that Mrs Amanda Phelan had seen washing his hands in a stream just after 10:30 on the morning of the murder as she was out walking three dogs belonging to friends. She, like Jane Harriman, was suspicious when she saw the man crouch in the water with his hands down as if rinsing them . . . 'I thought it was odd,' she said, 'but I couldn't get a good look at his face because he kept his head down.' The man, wearing what she thought was a cream or white sweater and blue jeans, stood up after a couple of seconds and then headed off in the direction of Putney Cemetery. She took the same route shortly afterwards and was spooked by her dogs suddenly barking furiously at the bushes near the graveyard. 'I thought somebody might be hiding in there. The dogs wouldn't behave like that otherwise,' she said.

Had Mrs Phelan seen the killer washing incriminating bloodstains from his hands or was it just another innocent walker refreshing himself on a warm summer day? A team of police officers searched every inch of the 200-yard route between the murder scene and the cemetery walls, scanning the land with metal detectors in case a knife had been thrown away or hidden. They found old knives, but none that matched the imprint left on Rachel's body. Curiously the only scent to have been picked up by a police tracker dog after the murder ran alongside the drainage ditch where the man was seen rinsing his hands and ended abruptly at the cemetery walls. It would not have been difficult, police realised, for a fit and active man to have scaled the wrought-iron railings at the cemetery's edge and made his escape through the huge graveyard.

The incident room was still working flat out, attempting to piece together the jigsaw of clues. Detectives were feeding the constant stream of information into nine computer terminals linked to HOLMES. Each incoming phone call was answered by one of a team of fourteen officers manning the hunt headquarters, with messages first taken down in longhand and then typed in as data. Chalked on blackboards around the room were the names of officers busy on the inquiry and which leads they were chasing and what progress they were making, as they waited hoping for a prime suspect to emerge. All around was an air of urgency. Amid the frenetic activity sat a large cuddly doll with red ears, a red nose and a yellow hat perched on its head. It had been sent by an unknown granny for little Alex in the hope that it could help to ease the pain of his loss. Upstairs was a cabinet full of more toys, all sent by people Alex would never know, their hearts and lives touched by his tragedy. Such was the compassion, the emotion, aroused by the murder.

Would Britton, Ressler and offender profiling be able to catch the heartless killer who had caused such sorrow? The process, familiar in America since 1957, had been used successfuly in Britain for ten years, most notably in the mid-eighties when Scotland Yard and three Home Counties police forces were hunting a double killer known as the Railway Rapist. Professor David Canter, of Surrey University's psychology department, drew up a profile of John Duffy, one of 1,999 suspects on the police computer. Because of his blood group, he was originally ranked only 1,505 on the list by detectives but shot to prime suspect position after Professor Canter produced a psychological profile which matched Duffy in thirteen of its seventeen points and persuaded police to put him under 24-hour surveillance. The operation yielded the evidence the police needed and Duffy, a martial arts fanatic who had stalked the railway systems for two years looking for victims, was jailed for life at the Old Bailey in 1988.

It had been something of a pioneering exercise by Professor Canter but proved so devastatingly successful that he subsequently set up a postgraduate course in investigative psychology at Surrey University, enabling both police and psychologists to study certain aspects of criminal behaviour in unison. Canter, who published the authoritative work *Criminal Shadows*, described profiling as often 'more of an art than a science. On a note of caution, he added 'Profilers can get it seriously wrong.' He cited the case of the Waco siege in Texas, which ended in disaster after America's finest FBI experts and psychological profilers had totally misinterpreted the probable reactions of religious crank David Koresh and his followers. Although Canter is rated among the leading exponents of profiling, he says realistically, 'Offender profiling does not solve crimes, only good police work does that.'

The technique was also used in the investigation into Michael Sams, the one-legged Midlands man who killed teenager Julie Dart and kidnapped estate agent Stephanie Slater. Paul Britton was among the expert witnesses at his trial at Nottingham Crown Court in 1993, when he was jailed for life. Britton's expertise led him to tell police that they should be looking for someone whose motivation was engaging the police in a deadly battle of wits, which turned out to be exactly Sams's macabre 'game'.

Altogether, offender profiling has been used in more than 100 cases in ten years, but used invariably as an aid to an investigation, not the very core of it as it was likely to be in the Rachel inquiry. A number of senior police officers urged caution in the use of the technique, warning that it should not be regarded as some sort of secret weapon against crime, able to produce suspects out of a hat. John Stevens, Chief Constable of Northumberland and co-ordinator in the field of offender profiling for the Association of Chief Police Officers, said, 'It should not be regarded as a magical concept which will categorically identify an offender. The huge publicity generated by its application to a few high-profile cases has tended to misrepresent offender profiling as a panacea for difficult cases.'

The British police were hoping to have an offender profiling database up and running some time in 1995. A lot would depend on the outcome of the Rachel Nickell inquiry.

The Wimbledon murder team were under no illusions. Whatever the arguments for and against, they realised that offender profiling was likely to be their greatest ally in the battle to find Rachel Nickell's killer. And they also knew that this was likely to be the toughest test yet for a concept still in its infancy.

The Biggest Wrench Imaginable

On the Alton Estate, Lillian Avid switched on her television with special interest on the evening of 17 September, two months and two days after the Rachel Nickell murder had happened so uncomfortably close to home. Virtually everyone on the sprawling development in Roehampton was tuned in. It was the night the BBC *Crimewatch* team were presenting a murder update and issuing new appeals in the hope of a much-needed breakthrough in the inquiry. An artist's impression of a man police suspected might be the killer was flashed on the screen. Mrs Avid sat bolt upright in her chair. 'That's just like Colin Stagg,' she exclaimed. She remembered all too well how she had seen Stagg in the street just hours after the murder, looking unusually excited, clean as if he'd just had a bath or shower, and saying how he had been on the common just ten minutes before Rachel died. Mrs Avid had asked him bluntly, 'Are you sure you didn't do it, Colin?' It seemed an odd accusation out of the blue but Mrs Avid had known Stagg for a couple of years as a quiet loner who, on normal occasions, would barely offer the time of day, and his sudden agitation over the murder had made her suspicious from the outset.

They had met originally at the Job Centre in Putney and saw each other maybe a couple of times a month as they walked their dogs to and from the Alton Estate for exercising on Wimbledon Common. 'We mostly spoke about the dogs, not much else,' she said. 'He certainly never spoke out of turn.' Yet there he was a couple of hours after the murder, rushing up and asking if she knew about the woman and child and saying he used to stand at the spot where it happened and look down on it. Mrs Avid thought to herself, 'How does he know where it happened?' She certainly didn't know the exact spot herself — although a neighbour had told her someone had been hurt somewhere on the common — and the whole area had been sealed off to the public since it happened. Mrs Avid was interested in keeping the usually reticent Stagg chatting for as long as she could. She told him he might have been in a position to help the woman if he'd been there a few minutes later. Stagg, visibly excited, replied in a monosyllabic 'yeah, yeah' — a response familiar to those on the estate who knew him. Mrs Avid decided to get straight to the point and asked him outright if he had anything to do with the murder. To her mind the response to such a stunning accusation was strange. Stagg just grinned and replied, 'Nah'. Mrs Avid felt edgy at the way he was behaving. There was definitely something odd about him that day.

Stagg was dressed in summery white T-shirt and white shorts, his hair looking neat and newly washed. 'He looked extra clean, immaculate,' she said. 'Even the clothing he was wearing looked new, it was all fresh,' said Mrs Avid. She was so perturbed at what she was feeling deep inside that she went home and telephoned her daughter in Kent for advice on what to do. 'I felt sick and ill and worried,' she said. 'I am a naturally nervous person and I was dubious as to whether to get involved or not.' However, a brief chat with her daughter reassured her that there was only one course of action. She telephoned Wimbledon police station, spoke to a woman officer in the incident room and waited for detectives to visit. No-one ever arrived. 'I just wasn't taken notice of,' she said. Not, at least, until many weeks later, on 17 September, when she saw that videofit — a computer enhancement of the artist's impression — on the TV screen. 'I was sick in my stomach, gutted,' she said. It was a remarkable likeness of Colin Stagg, the man she had told police about more than eight weeks earlier, when they had shown no interest.

She slept on it overnight and decided she must contact the police again the following day. She got up and went out in the morning, intending to sneak round to Stagg's home in Ibsley Gardens to check what number he lived at and then call Wimbledon police again. She was just about to knock on another door in the street to inquire about Stagg when he emerged three doors away. Startled, Mrs Avid asked him, 'Oh, where's your dog? Aren't you taking him for a walk?' Stagg told her he was simply going to the shops.

At that very moment a man stepped between them, took Stagg by the arm and said, 'I want to talk to you.'

Mrs Avid's assumption that he was a police officer was correct. He was quickly joined by a second detective. Both officers took close note of the inscription on Stagg's front door: 'Christians Keep Away. A Pagan Dwells Here'. Inside the three-bedroom maisonette — where he lived alone — police found a room painted black, rings of stones, a home-made altar and a pentagram and pagan drawings — all paraphernalia associated with witchcraft rituals. On the coffee table in the lounge was a copy of the *Daily Mirror* showing the Crimewatch videofit. 'Well, Colin, that looks a lot like you,' said Detective Inspector Pedder, nodding towards the picture.

'It's nothing like me,' retorted Stagg. 'I couldn't do a thing like that. She was a lovely girl. I saw her up there a couple of years ago. She smiled at me and we sat quite close together once near the Kingsmere Pond. But I never followed her.'

It was 12 noon on 18 September when Colin Stagg, 29 years old, unemployed, unmarried, living a hermit-like existence with only his dog Brandy for a friend, became chief suspect for the Rachel Nickell murder.

The Stagg family had lived on the Alton Estate for more than twenty years, with the five children — four brothers and a sister — attending local primary and comprehensive schools. Colin Stagg had complained of bullying as a lad, apparently over the way he walked, and had resolved to build up his skinny physique. None of the family shone academically, although Colin showed some talent as an artist and guitarist, and all duly drifted into a variety of mundane occupations. Their mother, Hilda, left her lazy and dominating husband, Vic, when Colin was in his early teens. Of all the Stagg children, Colin took it the worst. He made little effort to build bridges and rejected his mother's invitation to come to her new home for lemonade and pocket money. He remained loyal to his father and they shared a maisonette in Ilsley Gardens until 1986 when Vic Stagg suddenly died and Colin Stagg found himself alone. His long-suffering mother had by now found new happiness with ex-seaman David Carr, now a mini-cab driver, and set up home with him in a flat close to the Thames in Putney, just a few miles away from the Alton Estate. Colin Stagg was now living alone in a property suitable for an entire family, with no job, no commitments and his rent and overheads met by dole cheque and welfare payments. To many neighbours it seemed unaccountable that he should enjoy such relative luxury at the taxpayers' expense.

Amazingly, at the age of almost 30, he was still a virgin. The few girlfriends with whom he had attempted sex said he simply 'couldn't get it up'. In the Stagg family history, there was a suggestion of child abuse involving Victor and an eleven-year-old girl, son Anthony had been jailed in 1986 for raping a nineteen-year-old girl on Putney Heath and son Lee was into drugs. It was a family not without its problems.

If the psychologist and the FBI expert were right, Colin Stagg looked a textbook candidate for the offender profiling analysis of Rachel's killer. A quick confession, the police hoped, and it would all be over. However, far from being the end of the investigation, the arrest of Colin Stagg was just the beginning of a chapter in a police inquiry which would go on to make criminal and legal history.

Stagg was held at Wimbledon police station as detectives began a systematic search of his home and garden for evidence which might link him with the murder of Rachel Nickell. They realised that in the two months that had elapsed he could have destroyed any clothing or shoes that he might have been wearing. There were knives in the maisonette but none which bore any traces of blood; none which matched the wounds on Rachel's body.

Detective Inspector Pedder sat oppposite Colin Stagg in the interview room at Wimbledon police station that afternoon and pushed the start button for the tape recorder. He confirmed the names of the police officers present and the fact that Stagg's solicitor, Graeme Woods of Keith Hollis Woods, was there with a social worker representing the 'responsible adult' required to be in attendance in certain cases under the terms of the Police and Criminal Evidence Act, known simply to the police as PACE and introduced by the government in the eighties largely to safeguard the rights of arrested suspects.

'Have you got any outdoor pursuits, Colin?' asked Pedder.

'Yes, I like walking my dog,' Stagg replied. It was a

deliberately gentle start in the subtle battle between the two men.

'What sort of person are you?' asked the detective, a solid man with a moustache, who couldn't be anything but a policeman even if you put him in a Cup final crowd at Wembley.

'I'm a bit introverted,' Stagg replied quietly.

'You like to spend a lot of time by yourself, like your own company?'

'Yeah, me and my dog.'

Stagg told the police he remembered the day of the murder well because he had been suffering from a blinding headache and had a painful cramp in his neck. He'd taken Brandy the dog — given to him by neighbour Rita Nagy after his own faithful black labrador had died, causing him much distress — for a walk on the common at 8:30 a.m. He showed the police his route on a map of the common spread on the interview table. It was a shorter walk than usual, he said, because he felt so bad. 'I wanted to get back to get some sleep,' he told the detectives. 'I felt really drowsy.' He said he went straight back to Ibsley Gardens, munched a couple of crispbreads and fell asleep on the settee with some sort of game show, possibly hosted by Tom O'Connor, he couldn't remember exactly who, showing on the telly. He was woken later on by the noise of a police helicopter thundering overhead.

Could the police examine the shoes he was wearing that day, asked the detectives, anxious to try for a match with some of the prints they had found in the soil around Rachel's body. 'I threw them away two days ago,' said Stagg. 'They went into the bins in the block.'

Pedder glanced at his colleagues and knew it was not going to be easy.

For him, said Stagg, 15 July had been just another ordinary day and he certainly hadn't been out on the common murdering anyone. Up at 6:30 a.m. as usual — 'I haven't got an alarm, just a sort of body clock' — do a paper round for a local newsagent, walk the dog, eat his usual couple of Ryvita, buy some mince from the Co-op. Nothing could have been more normal. The first he knew of anything amiss was when he heard the helicopters and was told by local traders that there had been a murder.

What about the weird slogan on his front door? What did that mean? 'Oh, it's just to get rid of the bible bashers,' he said. And the black room with its pentagram, stones and symbols? Stagg paused for a second. 'It's not anything to do with Satan,' he said. It was, he explained, all part of his belief in the Wicca religion, an ancient philosophy which pre-dates Christianity by thousands of years. 'It's basically to do with the old religions, the pagan religions of Britain and Ireland,' he explained.

Then the man suspected of committing one of the most evil crimes the detectives had ever had the misfortune to become involved in began talking about the sanctity of life. The police officers listened intently. Stagg told them, 'It's our belief that all life is precious, all, like, y'know, like animal life. Everything has a spirit, y'know, trees, even rocks, even a breath of wind has got a spirit.'

Pedder looked at him quizzically. 'So you believe that all life is precious?' The image of Rachel Nickell's ravaged body was never far from his mind as he looked at the young man opposite talking about good and evil.

Stagg told the officers that so deep was his conviction of every creature's right to survive that he still lived with deep regret at killing spiders, ants and woodlice as a child.

What, asked Pedder, were the two knives used for which police had found at his home? The larger one, said Stagg, was for chopping wood, the smaller one for skinning rabbits, if the need ever arose on one of his backpacking trips or nature rambles. He went on, 'Although I admit taking a knife on my walks, if I wanted to skin an animal in a survival situation, to tell you the truth, I don't think I would. I feel that no matter how civilised we are, if you get caught up in a survival situation you'd have to do such things to survive. To tell you the truth I would feel guilty about killing even a little animal, but our ancestors have been doing it for thousands of years to survive.'

An extraordinary statement. Was this the devious mind of Rachel's killer cunningly covering his tracks with a smokescreen of quasi-religious claptrap — or a sad social misfit clinging to some intangible dogma to help to fill an otherwise empty existence? Pedder probed further. Yes, said Stagg, he had seen the *Crimewatch* programme the previous night. What was his reaction? 'When you came out with that description I thought, "That could be me",' he said. 'But he was over six feet tall. I'm not.'

Had he seen the evocative video shown on the programme of the happy, laughing Rachel Nickell cavorting with her young son? 'Quite poignant, wasn't it?' suggested Pedder, who had two young boys of his own safely tucked up at home. 'Yeah,' replied Stagg.

Had he ever seen her on the common during his many excursions there? 'I saw someone who could have been her about two years ago,' he said. 'She was pushing a little baby in a buggy. I was very skinny and pale at the time. She was lying by a pond with her kid and smiled at me. She was a nice-looking girl. I saw her take her top off and sunbathe in a bikini. I stayed for quite a while.'

Stagg said he remembered the incident well because at the time he was suffering from an illness caused by an allergy to flour and pasta dishes and wasn't feeling at his best. Nevertheless he went back on to the common the following day, hoping to see the woman again. 'When a girl smiles at you,' said Stagg in a sort of man-to-man way, 'I thought I could get chatting to her . . . you feel like your luck's in, you know.' Could it be, police now wondered, that Rachel had signed her own death warrant by smiling innocently at a passing stranger on Wimbledon Common and that she had become the object of a sexual obsession over the last two years?

Pedder probed deeper. 'You're a solitary sort of person?' he asked.

'Yes,' replied Stagg. 'I'm not really into people, y'know.'

Detective Constable Martin Long, another experienced officer on the murder team, continued to question Stagg the following day, concentrating on his special affinity with the common. It was clear that Stagg had a knowledge of the ancient park that was second to none. He knew the exact names of the hills, ponds, paths and woods and a great deal of their history — from the Curling Pond which Queen Victoria had arranged to be dug for the once popular winter sport of curling, to the triple mounds of Jerry's Hill, where highwayman Jerry Abershaw, who rode out from the Bald Stag in Kingston Vale, was gibbeted in 1795, and where Colin regularly fed a pair of semi-tame ravens. He took his dog Brandy out every day without fail, he said, even on visits to his dad's grave in Putney Cemetery. Never, he said, did he venture on to the common without his pet.

During his second day of questioning, Stagg remained adamant that he had risen at 6:30 a.m. as usual, done his paper round, walked the dog at 8:30 then gone back home for a snooze. It definitely wasn't until he was woken by the police helicopter, he maintained, that he went out, in shorts, T-shirt and sunglasses, for a second walk with Brandy, that he knew anything about the murder. He was stopped and told by a policeman at the A3 underpass that a girl had been killed on the common. 'I was shocked,' he told the police interviewers. 'I gave the officer my name and address and thought that would be it. Everything I have told you is the exact truth. I am not a murderer. I could never hit a woman even if I wanted to. I don't even hit my dog.'

No, he said emphatically, he was not the man seen by some witnesses on the day of the murder, carrying a black bag, with a belt or dog lead round his waist, and nor was he the man one woman had spotted washing his hands in a stream. 'I don't have a black bag,' he said, 'and I only take a bath on Thursdays and Sundays. It's routine. I've never washed my hands in the stream, it smells. If I did that I would smell.' He was equally adamant that he had not seen Rachel on the common that morning. 'I would have noticed someone like her. I had told a neighbour that I thought I had seen her two years ago with her baby in a buggy. I didn't see her, I swear on my dog's life. I couldn't kill her. Even when my dog does something wrong I can't even hit him.'

It became patently clear with each passing hour that Colin Stagg — if he was, indeed, the killer — was never likely to confess. His denials were persistent and emphatic. Two or three times Pedder and Long thought they had him on the ropes, that he was beginning to enmesh himself in a web of lies. Then the buzzer on the tape recorder would go, signalling the end of a half-hour period of interrogation. In the three or four minutes it took to take out the tape, label it, seal it so that it could not be tampered with and then place a new, clean tape in the machine, Stagg was able visibly to pull himself together, regain his composure and continue with the interview in total command of his faculties. Each time he came back, the police thought, he was like another man, adopting different attitudes, different postures. How the officers regretted that wretched buzzer and wondered when the day would come when interview tapes would be much, much longer.

Although there were no admissions from Stagg about the Rachel killing, he had made one startling confession during the twelve-hour police interrogation. He told the detectives he was a flasher! He agreed that he was the naked man seen by a startled woman wearing 'nothing but sunglasses and a smile' sometime between the day of the murder and 24 July, nine days later.

Held over a period of three days after police had obtained a court order for further detention, Stagg was duly charged with indecent exposure and whisked off next morning by squad car to Wimbledon Magistrates'

Court. The magistrates heard that a woman walking her dogs on the common's playing fields had seen Stagg lying completely naked, apart from sunglasses, with his clothes in a pile nearby. 'He opened his legs, exposing himself — and smiled,' said prosecutor Georgina Winfield. Stagg looked unconcerned, almost cocky, as the magistrates fined him £200 with £20 costs. The offence, said defence lawyer Graeme Wood in the packed courtroom, had nothing to do with the murder inquiry 'but because his name has been released to the press, his reputation has been sullied'.

Afterwards, Stagg tried to slip out of the rear doors of the court in a bid to escape the waiting group of reporters and photographers, all anxious to hear his comments about being held for three days as a suspect for the most horrific crime still outstanding in Britain at that time. Unfortunately for Stagg, the press contingent had done their homework and, instead of finding an escape route through the rear exit, he walked straight into a media ambush. He protested, 'I had nothing to be afraid of. I'm an innocent man and want to see the person who killed Rachel caught just as much as everyone else.' He then dashed off down the road, sticking a defiant two fingers up to cameramen.

Colin Stagg then returned to his home, his do-it-yourself pagan altar, his back-bedroom gymnasium, and his dog, branded a pervert but with the shadow of the Rachel Nickell murder inquiry apparently lifted. Scotland Yard said no further action would be taken against him. A day later they amended the position to say that Stagg had, in fact, been released on bail in respect of the Rachel inquiry and might still face further questioning.

In reality, Stagg was far from off the hook. Keith Pedder, for one, had a gut reaction that he was their man. However, in the current climate of headline-making dubious convictions, police had to be sure, above all else, that pure instinct did not put the wrong man in the dock. Hard, solid evidence was all that mattered and the file was looking threadbare in that department. There was certainly not enough to convince those at the Crown Prosecution Service that he should be charged with murder. A few days after Stagg's release, the police confirmed that they were anxious to trace Colin's brother, Tony, in connection with Rachel's murder. His rape conviction four years earlier, they decided, bore enough interesting similarities with the Rachel killing to warrant a closer look at a second member of the Stagg family. Tony's attractive nineteen-year-old victim had also been attacked while walking with a dog. It had happened on open land at Putney Heath, close to Wimbledon Common, very like the Rachel attack. And, police were told, Tony looked very like his brother Colin. For those reasons, said the detectives, they wished to question Tony with a view to eliminating him from inquiries. Tony Stagg was quickly traced to his home in Worcester and was able to provide a cast-iron alibi for his movements on the day Rachel died. It was another dead end in the hundreds of blind-alley leads followed up by Bassett and his police team. They desperately needed a breakthrough if they were ever going to see a successful conclusion to a frustratingly difficult case.

One consolation was that little Alex was making good progress towards normality, under the caring wing of leading child psychiatrist Dr Jean Harris Hendriks, supported by the love of his devoted father, his grandparents and the warmth of close friends whose own young children were playing a major part in healing the emotional scars. As the only witness to the murder, should Alex be shown photofits, videofits, photographs or film of any suspects? If so, how should it be done without reawakening the horror? After all, the little boy's reaction to a picture of Colin Stagg might tell the police everything they wanted to know, one way or another. Expert opinion was against it. He was only three. If the remarkable healing powers of nature could somehow ease those dreadful memories, or even wipe them out forever, then surely they should be allowed to do so. Perhaps just scattering an assortment of photographs on the table, including any suspects, and asking Alex if he could see anyone who had hurt his mummy might be a suitable compromise. The exercise was to have surprising results. Alex, in fact, named a close personal friend of Andre and Rachel's as 'the man who hurt Mummy'. Police inquiries revealed that the friend, called Andy, was thought by some of Rachel and Alex's acquaintances to be obsessed with her. He was a near neighbour and was quickly traced and interviewed by the top team of Pedder and Wickerson. He agreed he was extremely fond of Rachel, that he had sometimes accompanied her on walks with young Alex, but assured the officers that his was no *Fatal Attraction* relationship and he would never dream of harming her in any way. He was as shocked as anyone at the awful way in which she had died. Most importantly, he was able to provide a watertight alibi for his movements on the day Rachel was killed. He was totally eliminated from inquiries and the police were left pondering on Alex's words.

Colin Stagg had, in fact, been named by no fewer than four different people as a result of the *Crimewatch* appeal. He suddenly found the Alton Estate rife with hostility. He was verbally abused in the street. Women crossed the road to avoid close contact. There were even catcalls of 'murderer' from some. Stagg's already limited circle of friends dwindled to just one or two, prepared to give him the benefit of the doubt. Amid the storm, Stagg sought consolation in his pal Brandy, whose devotion was never in question as they continued their thrice-daily strolls across the common, remaining apparently oblivious to the public vilification. His loyal mum and stepdad never believed for one second that he could be the fiend who had brought such mayhem to Wimbledon Common.

Andre, alone in a world of grief, was spending every waking hour with his son, taking him on walks with Molly the dog, playing in the park, anything which reminded him of how things used to be. He still lived, and always will live, with a permanent horror film running through his mind of the moment he knew Rachel was gone forever. He had made a delivery in Cheshunt and decided to give Rachel a call at home, knowing she would just have got back from her walk on the common. He told writer Lynda Lee-Potter in the *Daily Mail*:

> 'There was a phone kiosk at the side of the road. I stopped my bike, went to the phone, dialled the number and a male voice answered. I thought I'd got the wrong

number, so I rang again, but I was thinking to myself, "I didn't dial the wrong number." Also something about his voice seemed odd. I heard the same man again say, "Who are you?" and I said, "It's Andre. Who are you?" It was going through my mind really quickly that something was terribly wrong. I'd gone cold completely. I started to feel ill. He said, "I'm a police officer." Your bowels just turn into ice, your legs go and your head spins. He said, "Where are you? Are you on your own? Who's with you?" and I said, "What's happened?" He said, "There's been an accident." I said, "Are they dead?" As I spoke the world was just beginning to spin in my head and he told me, "There's been a terrible accident." I said again, "Are they dead?" He said, "I can't tell you over the phone." I said, "I've got to know. I've got to know," and he said, "She's been killed." I said, "What about Alex?" He said, "He's all right, he's not been harmed." I said, "What happened to Rachel?" He said she had been attacked while walking on Wimbledon Common, that she had been killed, and I just wailed like an animal. He was desperately asking where I was, saying, "Don't move, we'll get a police car to you, just tell me where you are." I heard him say, "Just keep talking to me," and I said, "I've got to go" and put the phone down. I somehow managed to call my mother and wailed again. Then I leant on my bike and just wept and wept. People were walking past me, I thought I was going insane. I didn't hold out any hope that it was all a hoax, that Rachel had been badly injured, or that she'd recover. I knew she was dead, I knew it was true.'

The little boy caught up in all this emotional turmoil had remained amazingly calm after his initial trauma. But how do you tell a tot like that that Mummy's never coming home? Andre went to the hospital where Alex was being treated so sympathetically, carrying his favourite sheepskin rug under his arm, and walked down the corridor just as his son came walking towards him. 'He was calm. He was walking normally,' said Andre.

'He saw me and said, "Daddy". I ran towards him, picked him up, gave him his blanket. I expected him to be breaking down or whatever but he just looked numb. I said, "There's been a terrible accident. Mummy's been killed. She's never coming back. We're not going to see her again, but we're going to be all right, we're going to be OK. I'm here, Grandma's here, Mark's here, Molly's at the police station. We'll go and get Molly. We'll go back to Grandma's house. I've got everything you want." I was just putting on the cheerleader act. He stared at me and I knew from the way he looked that he knew Rachel had gone. He knew she was dead in a

way that I didn't. It just made perfect sense,
really, because he'd seen what had happened
to her.'

Alex slept soundly that night, his little body
weakened by shock. Andre, on the other hand, stayed up
all night with friends. 'I felt my insides had been ripped
out. It was just the biggest wrench, the biggest pain you
could ever imagine,' he recalled.

For vastly different reasons, Colin Stagg and Andre
Hanscombe, two men who were poles apart, would
remember 15 July 1992 for the rest of their lives.

The Trap is Set

Julie Pines recognised the name immediately. Colin Stagg, that was the name of the man who had answered her lonely hearts ad in *Loot* magazine. The man whose letters became so obscene that she never wrote back again. That was two years ago and, as far as she was concerned, it was good riddance. Now here he was in the papers as a suspect for the Wimbledon Common murder. What should she do? She thought long and hard about the implications and realised that she must tell the police. Perhaps it was nothing, but it had bothered her at the time. Lonely hearts ads can invite the attention of all sorts of weirdos; it's an occupational risk. But this guy had been right over the top, like someone hooked on kinky sex, writing fantasy letters about sex on Wimbledon Common. She found the number for Wimbledon police incident office and picked up the phone.

Julie Pines' call to the police in the autumn of 1992 changed the whole course of the inquiry. The filth Stagg had written in only the third letter of his brief correspondence with Julie could only have been conjured up by someone obsessed with the outer fringes of sexuality or with the most fertile and warped of imaginations. The detectives studied the five-page tirade of obscenity which factory worker Julie had reluctantly kept hidden away at her south London home after initially wanting to tear it up and throw it in the bin. It told how Stagg imagined he had been masturbating naked on the common when an attractive woman surprised him but, instead of being horrified, she had invited him to take part in a sordid outdoor sex romp. There were, thought the police, definite echoes of the Rachel Nickell case here. They showed it to psychologist Paul Britton, whose highly trained mind and years of experience told him that these were, indeed, the outpourings of a man displaying the kind of characteristics he had seen before in the most worrying of cases. It was time, the police decided, to get inside the mind of Colin Stagg.

Keith Pedder came up with what seemed like a master stroke of inspiration which was to propel the Rachel Nickell investigation into new realms of crime detection — 'Let's put an undercover policewoman in as a new pen pal for Stagg to see how he reacts.' He might, reasoned the officer, commit his innermost thoughts, his fears, his fantasies and his secrets to paper. Who knows, if it was totally successful, he might even confess his involvement in Rachel's murder. Alternatively, if he was innocent as he claimed, it would give him a chance to clear his name once and for all and allow the police to concentrate their activities in other areas.

Paul Britton agreed to mastermind the operation and assured the police that if Stagg was Rachel's killer he was almost certain to react in one way but if he was an innocent man he would react in another way altogether. It was an idea the police knew would be fraught with dangers, legal, professional, and perhaps physical if Stagg were to take the bait and form a 'romantic' relationship with the policewoman. Pedder bounced the idea off the senior officers involved in the inquiry, up to commander level at Scotland Yard. Yes, they said, it was a potentially brilliant tactical ploy which could take them behind Colin Stagg's so far impenetrable façade. But what about the problems of entrapment, enticement, acting as an agent provocateur — whatever heading it came under it was sure to become meat and gravy for a hungry defence lawyer. There was no point in pursuing the secret operation if the Crown Prosecution Service was likely to rule it unethical and therefore inadmissible as evidence in a court of law. Senior CPS lawyers, representing the best legal brains in Britain, were consulted. To the delight of the murder squad they gave it the go ahead. At last the police team had a solid line of inquiry, with at least some hope of a result at the end of it. Already, towards the end of 1992, from on high at Scotland Yard there had been rumblings of running down the inquiry. With the failure of the CPS to back a murder charge being brought against Stagg after the September arrest, senior officers at the Yard were pessimistic about continuing an operation which had no realistic prospect of bringing about a successful conviction and thought the money could be better spent elsewhere. The Wimbledon team were dismayed at the thought of abandoning the investigation at this stage, especially as Stagg had gone straight to a firm of lawyers after his detention in September and instructed them to sue the squad for wrongful arrest. He was sitting back and hoping for a handsome payout from police coffers.

It was essential that any covert operation devised by the murder team should be run hand in glove with psychologist Britton, who had drawn up the detailed profile of their killer soon after the murder and who would be able to identify significant behaviour patterns in Colin Stagg. Britton's expertise and clinical analysis would give the operation the authenticity it required if it was to stand up to scrutiny in court. Ultimately, the police hoped, if it was totally successful it could lead to the discovery of material evidence, like the murder knife, or soiled clothing, that would provide incontrovertible evidence for a jury. All that was needed was a policewoman with the skill and the courage to carry it off. Enter Detective Constable Lizzie James, Scotland Yard's foremost expert in undercover work, experienced in the field of drugs, terrorism and fraud, married to a former police officer. She knew the case well and had no hesitation in volunteering for a job which, she realised only too well, could take her into an unknown world of extreme sexual deviancy and might eventually bring her face to face with a man suspected of committing one of the most dreadful and demented murders in years.

So, under a cloak of the greatest secrecy, Operation Edzell was launched in the late autumn of 1992. The police decided it would look too obvious if Lizzie were to start writing to Stagg too quickly after the blaze of publicity surrounding his release from custody and appearance in court on the indecency charge. It was decided to let the situation calm down naturally and for Stagg to resume his normal lifestyle, or what passed for normal to him. Mr Britton, meanwhile, was asked to employ his professional skills in guiding the policewoman in what she should say in her opening letters to Stagg, in order to interest him but not entice him in that first crucial contact. Like a chess player with the gift of foresight, the psychologist predicted how Stagg could be expected to react at each stage of the operation if he was the killer and how he might behave if he wasn't. Either way, at the end of the operation, he assured the police, they would know whether or not they had the right man. The killer of Rachel Nickell, the psychologist emphasised, was suffering from the rarest form of uncontrollable sexually deviant abnormality, present in only one in around two and a half million of the male population. Was Stagg suffering from that same terrifying abnormality? The psychologist had listened closely to the police tape recordings of the interviews with Stagg after his arrest in September. He considered it 'highly significant' that Stagg had admitted being on Wimbledon Common close to the time of the murder. Britton had also read the vile Stagg letter to Julie Pines.

That too, displayed characteristics likely to be found in the mind of a sexual deviant, he said. If Stagg wasn't the killer of Rachel Nickell, said Britton, the undercover operation should provide an opportunity for him to eliminate himself from inquiries and throw off the shadow of suspicion for good. The Britton plan was to 'chart a course' (his own words) in which Stagg, if he were the killer, would admit his sexual desires for the domination and humiliation of women, would confess his bizarre and violent sexual fantasies and would finally incriminate himself in Rachel's murder with his own words and deeds.

Operation Edzell became Scotland Yard's best-kept secret in the knowledge that any leak could jeopardise the operation and, ultimately, the entire investigation. Only senior detectives and a hand-picked team of officers, appointed as Lizzie's invisible bodyguards in case of problems, were briefed.

Lizzie's first letter dropped through Colin Stagg's letterbox at 16 Ibsley Gardens in January 1993. She told him she was writing because she was a friend of 28-year-old Julie, his former lonely hearts penfriend, and wondered if he might like to write to her instead. She was, she said, a 'cat sitter' who moved around the country minding animals while their owners were away. Julie, she said, was all right but a bit of a prude, not broadminded like her. It was chatty, non-committal, another lonely heart looking for a soulmate, but just tantalising enough to get Stagg interested. The police knew that the first letter was all-important, that one false move could easily arouse Stagg's suspicions and halt the operation dead in its tracks. They knew Stagg was an animal lover and the use of a cat minder as cover for Lizzie was a subtle bonding — as well as a handy explanation for the different telephone numbers she might use in future contact with him and an excuse for not being able to invite him over because she was in someone else's home. It was a sensible tactic, enabling Lizzie to conduct the early stages of the operation at a safe distance.

Stagg sent his replies to an address Lizzie had given in Slough, Buckinghamshire, unaware, of course, that it was an accommodation address the police had rented to substantiate Lizzie's cover story. Stagg was cautious at first and wanted to know about her relationship with Julie Pines and why she had suddenly decided to write to him out of the blue. Lizzie's reply — written with Julie's assistance — seemed to satisfy Stagg that she was genuine. He had taken the bait. It was important from now on, said Britton, for Stagg to be allowed to make the running, that nothing Lizzie wrote should lead him on, and positively no mention should be made of the Rachel Nickell murder unless it was introduced by Stagg himself.

Paul Britton predicted that Stagg would quickly want to progress from mere letter writing to dates with Lizzie and ultimately physical contact with her. The police, he predicted, could have a result one way or the other as quickly as within eight weeks. The history of Lizzie James was to be that she had been a passive participant in the sexual murder of a young woman and baby some twelve years earlier, that she had later withdrawn from the group involved in a state of mental confusion, could only enter fully into a relationship with a man who had had similar experiences, and it was only after considerable thought that she was considering entering a new relationship at all. However, any details of her fictitious background were only to be released to Stagg bit by bit when circumstances were right and when he was prepared to 'trade' experiences.

The early exchange of letters, in January and February, introduced an atmosphere of soft porn into the relationship with Lizzie telling Stagg, 'I bet this is just the tip of the iceberg. There is more to you than meets the eye . . . you are obviously as broadminded as I am. I can't wait for your next letter. I'm sure your fantasies know no bounds . . .' The intensity began to build, with the police team drafting the Lizzie letters under Paul Britton's guidance and the psychologist analysing each letter Stagg returned. Lizzie sent him a Valentine card and a photo of herself . . . attractive, in her twenties, fair hair, the sort of girl the police suspected Stagg yearned for in his fantasy world. Stagg responded with jewellery and trinkets for Lizzie. She sent back a small Saisho personal hi-fi radio, paid for out of police funds. They had long, intimate telephone calls and, later, lunch in Hyde Park. They looked for all the world like a pair of young lovers. Only the undercover police watching their every movement knew the truth.

It soon became patently obvious to the squad that not only had Stagg swallowed the bait hook, line and sinker but he had also become totally infatuated with his dream girl. He wrote to Lizzie:

'My whole life now seems complete since you first wrote. I dream that I hold your little handies in mine and you start to blush as I tell you "I have fallen in love with you Lizzie, so much". I place myself between your legs and start to ease myself into your vaginal opening. I hope this relationship never ends.'

He followed up by telling Lizzie: 'I know I said I could be a bit possessive, but only because I've never really had anyone in my life to cherish and love, especially someone as beautiful as you . . . When I first got your letter I couldn't believe my luck . . . It was a dream come true . . . it only happens to other people. I hope everything's alright between us. Maybe I'm just being silly. I want us to go steady and have a long lasting relationship. I hope you want that too . . .'

The simple sentimentality eventually gave way to the first of a series of detailed sexual fantasies involving male domination and female submission. His letters were sometimes accompanied by crude, lavatory-wall sketches of a man and woman in sexual positions. The drawings were invariably dominated by a vicious-looking dagger at the top and featured huge penises, women lying down with their legs apart displaying their genitals, and couples making love doggy-fashion, with arrows pointing to the participants and the words 'Colin' and 'Lizzie' scrawled beside them. The dagger, said Paul Britton, was highly significant in the exchanges.

The operation was moving in the right direction and expectations were raised at Wimbledon HQ. It was clear that Colin Stagg had begun waiting eagerly for each new letter to arrive. After receiving one of the porn letters, Lizzie told him:

'Your lovely fantasy letter was absorbing. I only hope these are your genuine thoughts. I want it to be proven and true, not the usual sort of things everyone reads in magazines. My fantasy knows no bounds. My imagination runs riot. It would be nice to know if you have the same unusual dreams as me. I hope I'm not sounding unnatural. I sometimes scare myself with what I really want. Sometimes normal things just aren't enough. My demands are greater. I don't just mean straight sex, there is so much more to explore. God, please don't think I am a weirdo. Sexually people do not use their imagination. I'm sure you do, and can, Colin. Tell me something that will really drive me crazy . . . I constantly think about the letter you gave me at our first meeting where you took charge of the situation. You were manly and really showed me who is boss. I need someone like that, someone strong and powerful. I want you to take charge. You know yourself you are a man's man.'

It was a carefully calculated invitation to Stagg to unburden his most volatile emotions. Britton predicted that if he was the Nickell killer he would soon begin to throw caution to the wind and confide to Lizzie his very darkest desires. Stagg wrote to Lizzie telling her:

'Not only are you beautiful but like me you have a great open mind about sex. You agree with me some people have very boring outlooks. When we start to see each other regularly we will produce so much electricity between us we will probably explode. I assure you the fantasies I write are specially for you. I do read magazine stories of course but compared to my fantasies they are very tame. I sleep in the small bedroom on a sofa bed. I like doing DIY. It gives me great satisfaction. I finished the living room last year with new carpets and curtains. When you come round I hope you will like it. I know I'm unemployed, but I use it to my advantage to get things done. Don't worry, I'm not a lazy git. During the summer I do jobs like gardening.'

With the letter, Stagg included what he says is one of his favourite fantasies. 'I've invited you round for the evening. I've cooked you a meal of rice bolognaise followed by my own homemade raspberry mousse. There's soft lighting and romantic music as I sit waiting for your knock on the door . . . I want to tease you... I want to press my face into your vagina . . .'

As part of the carefully structured plan Lizzie hinted to Stagg in her next letter that she was troubled by happenings in her past. She told him:

'There are secrets about me I long to share. I've things to tell you you won't believe. I need to overcome this with you. Once this is done we'll be together forever. Things have happened to me which make my outlook totally different in every way, things which have changed my urges and responses.

Sometimes I feel guilty about the way I feel. You ask me to explain about how I feel when you write me letters. They excite me greatly, but I can't help feeling you are showing restraint. You are showing control, even when you feel like bursting. I want you to burst. I want you to feel you are all powerful and overwhelming so I'm completely in your power, defenceless and humiliated. These thoughts are sending me into paradise already. I've had my way too long. I need you to sort me out. I'm sure you are man enough to do it. Gulp, deep breath. I'm getting carried away. I think I had better go and have a cold shower.'

Stagg, ever waiting for the sound of his letterbox with more mail from Lizzie, clearly had no idea he was corresponding with an experienced police officer. The operation was running more smoothly than the police could ever have hoped. The intensity of his language grew with each exchange. His letters became peppered with the crudest of four-letter words. He talked of masturbating until he was 'red raw', of performing every conceivable sex act with Lizzie. It was, said Paul Britton, precisely the sort of reaction he would expect from the killer of Rachel Nickell. Stagg wrote back to Lizzie after she had sent a letter to him in mid-March:

'Your letter was great. I've now some idea of what you want. I hope you aren't offended by the dirty names I call you. I don't think you are any of those things. I hope we will be good friends and that we will have a great relationship and will fall in love. I want to dominate you, take your body as my plaything. The things I am going to do to you will make your eyes water. I want to say things to you while abusing your body. I want to call you names. You will be left humiliated and dirty. You are going to feel sore and exhausted. Lizzie, I'm going to make you pay for what you have done to me. I'm going to make sure you are screaming in agony when I abuse you. I'm going to destroy your self-esteem. You will never look anybody in the eye again. I hope you enjoyed my last letter. Was that the kind of thing you want? If you find it too offensive, especially calling you names, I can't apologise enough.'

It was now patently clear what drove Stagg's sexual desires. But how much was just fantasy? Could he have turned his perverted desires into horrifying reality that day on Wimbledon Common? The police were becoming increasingly suspicious that Colin Stagg was their man.

Stagg told Lizzie of his belief in the pagan religion and wrote, 'If you have beliefs of your own, I respect that. I would not force my beliefs on anyone. Each to his own I say.' She told him:

'In the past my beliefs have involved other people. I don't see any of these other people now and have not done so for some time as certain things we did together made me have mixed feelings. Don't worry, I'll tell you the full story some day soon. This has made me feel empty and alone . . . I often recall those times.'

Stagg was quick to pick up on the implications. 'Am I right in saying you practised sexual rituals?' he asked. 'If that's what you are trying to tell me, don't worry. I've always wanted to practise that.' To indicate his commitment to his pagan beliefs, he sent Lizzie a cheap talisman, shaped like an eye, in the post in the second week of April. And he asked more about Lizzie's past secrets, clearly fascinated at what may have befallen her.

She told him: 'The things that happened when I was with this man were not what normal people would like. These involved upsetting and often hurting people. Even now these things are bad and I ought to feel guilty but I cannot forget how exhilarated they made me feel. I'm keen to feel the same way, but not by hurting others.'

Stagg revealed to Lizzie the contents of the letter which had so shocked Julie Pines . . . his urge for open-air sex, with the risk of being casually observed, and of his desire for domination over his female partner. Stagg's correspondence — usually neatly handwritten in capital letters — also roamed into the areas of woodland sex and mentioned a log and a stream . . . all characteristics which featured very prominently in the Rachel Nickell murder. In one, possibly all-revealing phrase, he told Lizzie that women made fun of him and made him feel small. He said he felt lonely and unwanted when he saw young couples together on Wimbledon Common. These, thought the police, were the utterings of a man with misogyny in his mind. Increasingly, Stagg asserted that he and Lizzie would soon have a 'pain and pleasure sex session together'. He was clearly highly excited at the prospect. He was beginning to open up to Lizzie as the psychologist had predicted. At murder hunt headquarters hopes were high that the major breakthrough they so dearly needed was just around the corner.

When Stagg sent Lizzie the witchcraft talisman, he said it would protect her from the thoughts of 'closed-minded people'. Lizzie, sticking to the 'script' of Paul Britton, had intimated to Stagg that her troubled past, steeped in the occult, had involved the ritual murder of a young girl. She told him of a deep, intense relationship with another man over a six-year period when she was aged between twelve and eighteen.

Stagg, by now overwhelmed with desire for Lizzie, sent a letter containing a gold ring like some unofficial engagement gift, and clearly indicating his willingness to carry on the relationship despite the fact his pen pal had confessed to being a party to murder.

Careful thought was given to arranging face-to-face meetings between the girl detective and the prime suspect who had become so besotted with her. It was dangerous and delicate territory.

For that reason the police chose The Dell restaurant, beside London's Serpentine Lake in Hyde Park, as a suitable venue, holding probably fewer dangers than many others. It was relatively open, was normally busy with the tourist trade and could be watched without arousing too much suspicion. That first meeting was an eerie experience for Lizzie James. She had kissed her husband goodbye that morning and then headed for a date with a man who might possibly have committed a murder which had outraged the nation and who, by his own admissions to date, took pleasure in the violent sexual domination of women. Now, here they were at midday, laughing and chatting like innocent young lovers It was Lizzie's finest role — and probably her most important to date — in her career as an undercover police officer.

Her Scotland Yard bosses had ensured, as far as was humanly possible, that her safety would not be compromised. At no stage in the operation, they ruled, must there be fewer than 30 other plain-clothes officers watching her and Stagg's every move. Lizzie knew that the apparent strangers sitting nearby were reliable colleagues ready to spring to her assistance if circumstances dictated. Stagg suspected nothing, particularly the fact that his pretty companion, whose face and figure he looked at so intently, was wired for sound, a tiny hidden microphone sending every word of their conversation to a sophisticated tape recorder. Even amid this tense drama Lizzie found time to play a sly joke on one of her watching colleagues, sitting innocuously at the next table, looking for all the world like another hungry tourist enjoying lunch. From her handbag Lizzie pulled a small camera, called a Sneaky Snapper, and asked her fellow undercover officer sweetly: 'Will you take a photo of us together, please?' The detective, taken completely by surprise, still managed to look nonchalant as he took the camera, pointed it at Lizzie and Stagg and asked them to smile as he fired off a shot. 'Thank you very much,' she smiled as she put the camera back in her bag. Stagg remained totally unaware that he had been set up for a vital picture which would go into the police evidence file.

'It was a little bit wicked of Lizzie to spring it on one of our team like that,' said one of her colleagues, 'but that's her sense of humour. It might have been a bit risky with less experienced officers but this team knew exactly what they were doing.'

With lunch over, Stagg handed another of his now notorious fantasy letters to Lizzie as they chatted and sipped coffee. The theme, once again, was the crying urge in his life to dominate and humiliate the opposite sex. The fantasy detailed a pretty, fair-haired girl being abused by hair pulling, knife threats and verbal assault, culminating in violent sex with blood dripping from the woman's nipples. It was gruesome reading in the Hyde Park sunshine. Lizzie feigned interest. Stagg became so visibly excited sexually that it was embarrassing to others in the restaurant, a fact clearly witnessed by other surveillance officers. Stagg seemed oblivious to any discomfort that his erection caused Lizzie or anyone else. His fantasy world seemed to be dominating his life to the exclusion of all else. This, said Paul Britton, was entirely consistent with the kind of vivid masturbatory repertoire he would expect to find in the killer of Rachel Nickell. It indicated once again that the suspect, Stagg, fitted in with that tiny fraction of sexual deviants who might be capable of committing a murder like that of Rachel Nickell.

Lizzie's lifestyle had been turned on its head by her involvement with Colin Stagg, but never once did she ever consider opting out of her role. Quite deliberately, she was never allowed access to some of the more detailed aspects of Rachel's murder, in particular to the highly specialised reports of the pathologist Dr Shepherd and Paul Britton. It was felt that she should have only the basic information, such as any member of the public would have gleaned from newspaper and TV reports, in case she inadvertently dropped something of a specialised police nature into conversations, which would alert Stagg and send him scuttling off before the operation was complete.

By the time Operation Edzell had entered its fifth month — and with the overall investigation costing well in excess of a million pounds — authority was needed at the highest level to continue with Lizzie's infiltration. Senior Scotland Yard officers, murder team leaders, CPS lawyers and Paul Britton met for a confidential briefing and update on the prospects of an arrest. With the evidence emerging from the Lizzie inquiry — frustratingly slow as it was at times — there were clear grounds for continuing with the undercover operation, argued Pedder and Wickerson. If it led to a successful conclusion in such a prominent murder investigation, they maintained, it would have been worth every penny, not least in the area of public confidence. The Yard chiefs had little hesitation in giving the Wimbledon team the green light to carry on with Operation Edzell. It proved a fruitful decision. Two weeks later, Stagg told Lizzie for the first time that he had been arrested on suspicion of the Rachel Nickell murder. It was, he said, as a result of mischief-making by lying neighbours on the Alton Estate. He told Lizzie he was not implicated in the killing in any way. And, he claimed, he had been wrongly convicted of exposing himself to a woman on Wimbledon Common — all part of a campaign of victimisation by the police.

Lizzie and Stagg continued their extraordinary 'courtship', with the WPC's letters, tapes and conversations adding hundreds of pages to the police evidence file and Stagg remaining apparently unaware that he was a target in a huge and complex charade. The sexually laden telephone calls from Stagg, made from ordinary call boxes, sometimes from open-sided booths with little privacy, were analysed by the ever-cool Paul Britton, who delivered his clinical judgements on their contents in his normal, quiet, unexcitable manner. This was not a job Britton enjoyed. He did it, unpaid, for the simple satisfaction of helping the police in difficult inquiries.

In one notable tape, Lizzie, pretending to be equally as enthusiastic as Stagg at the prospect of violent sex, told him it might be easier for her to unburden her mind to him if he was the killer of Rachel Nickell. She might then be able to reveal her tormented past and its violent memories to someone who would truly understand her emotional agonies. It was, on the face of it, almost an indirect accusation of murder, certainly the offering of a confessional shoulder. Stagg showed little sign of concern, but, following their next meeting, Paul Britton formed the opinion that Stagg was becoming extremely cautious. Had he smelled a rat? No, said the psychologist, he did not think the operation was in danger. The explanation, he said, would be consistent with the killer of Rachel Nickell taking stock of his position to date, wanting to hold back for his own protection, yet at the same time anxious to progress further with the relationship with Lizzie James. Britton predicted that he might soon either reveal a connection with the Rachel murder or, alternatively, fabricate a story to match that of

Lizzie and the grotesque secret he believed she harboured in her past. It was an uncanny prediction.

A few days later, Stagg told Lizzie that he had not murdered Rachel but had been involved, with his cousin, in the murder of a young girl and that they had hidden her body in the New Forest. He gave Lizzie grisly details with apparent relish and said, 'I've never told anyone else about that in my life.' Britton's interpretation was that Stagg might have interwoven details of the Rachel Nickell murder into his fictional account of the New Forest killing. It was another firm pointer to the belief that the police were aiming in the right direction.

In another animated call to Lizzie, soon after, Stagg talked lasciviously about sexual entry from the rear during intercourse — another feature of Rachel's murder. Slowly the evidence was mounting but it was still only circumstantial and largely academic, not something that was going to impress a judge and jury. There were the Crown Prosecution Service and a magistrate still to convince yet before they were remotely close to seeing Colin Stagg standing in the dock of the Central Criminal Court on a murder charge.

Early in June, Lizzie and Stagg met again. Stagg was becoming ever more insistent that she should come to his home in Roehampton — clearly anticipating a sexual encounter — and gave her a map showing her exactly how to get there. Again, however, he was showing abnormal caution. How could he be sure she was genuine, he asked. He said he had trusted people before but had been badly let down and that was why he was facing problems over the Rachel Nickell murder.

Because of Stagg's suspicions about her true identity, it was decided that Lizzie should send him some of her own fantasies to convince him that she was someone of a like mind. Her letters — in fact, joint works from the minds of Mike Wickerson, Keith Pedder and the officers at Wimbledon — detailed fantasies involving animals and submissive sex but carefully did not inject more violence or depravity than that already explored by Stagg himself in earlier correspondence. He phoned to say thanks, seemingly convinced that Lizzie was, indeed, genuine.

They met again in Hyde Park at the end of June and it proved to be the most rewarding encounter so far. Stagg, confident once again, said he would like to enact a bizarre kidnap and rape scene with Lizzie in the starring role. She would be held at knifepoint and anally raped, said Stagg. Most significantly, he said he wanted their next meeting to be on Wimbledon Common because it was so much quieter than Hyde Park. The conversation turned to the Rachel murder. Stagg told her that he had, in fact, been on the common at the time and was still sexually aroused at the thought of what had happened to Rachel. Lizzie's pulse quickened. Stagg said he wanted to take her to the murder site but was deterred by the possibility of police surveillance cameras. Stagg then described injuries suffered by Rachel in precise detail — the exact position of her body, the distribution of blood in the area. He gave graphic descriptions of her vaginal and anal areas after the attack, claiming to have seen a police photo during his detention at Wimbledon police station.

He told Lizzie: 'I could see her cunt in that. He really forced her open, you know. He was obviously killing her at that time . . . The muscles, or whatever, in her body, you know, and that made her stay open.' He continued his sickening diatribe by telling Lizzie that he had got sexual arousal from seeing the police pictures of Rachel's corpse. It took all Lizzie's professional self-control to remain emotionally detached from such unmitigated callousness. As evidence, the police believed it was dynamite. The murder squad detectives were sure Stagg had never seen photos of Rachel at the murder HQ which would have given him anything like the insight he now claimed to have.

Police organised another high-level case conference to consider their next move. Any doubts that Colin Stagg was just a sick pervert and nothing more were evaporating by the minute. The man knew too much, the police thought.

Stagg, now under almost constant but careful surveillance, continued to bombard Lizzie with phone calls, written fantasies and requests for her to visit his home or Wimbledon Common. Sometimes he confessed to being so excited by their conversations that he had to put down the phone and dash back home to masturbate. That would have been done, police felt sure, in the DIY gymnasium in his bedroom, bedecked with dozens of sordid 'meat slab' pin-up pictures taken from magazines at the seedier end of the porn market.

Stagg, the detectives believed, had now thrown caution to the wind and, with careful manipulation, was ready to confess all to Lizzie James. All it would take, they anticipated, was one fateful visit to the common to bring the memories flooding back and trigger his desperate urge to say, 'Yes, it was me.' It was only a matter of time.

Britton's clinical evaluation of Stagg backed a hundred per cent the police belief that he was the killer of Rachel Nickell. The psychologist in the gold-rimmed glasses could never professionally say, 'I am certain Stagg is the murderer,' but he told the Wimbledon officers that Stagg's behaviour was 'entirely consistent' with that of the man who had so brutally butchered Rachel Nickell. The likelihood of someone else with the same deviant traits being on the common at the same time were very slim indeed.

It was exactly what the police wanted to hear. Their man was in their sights. Here was a police squad now entirely convinced by the merits of offender profiling and its uncannily accurate diagnosis of the sickest members of our society. Keith Pedder, who had spent five and a half years chasing hard-case villains across London as part of the Flying Squad's crack Tower Bridge robbery unit, now became a card-carrying supporter of the new crimefighting expertise. So intent did his involvement become that he struck up a close personal friendship with Paul Britton and travelled to the USA with him to study FBI techniques in offender profiling at Quantico. So impressed were the FBI with Pedder that they asked him to take a knowledge-sharing and educational secondment with them. However, his Scotland Yard bosses ruled that that could not happen until after the Stagg case was closed. There was the final mile still to go for Rachel Nickell.

A quiet air of confidence hung over the incident room as the first anniversary of Rachel's murder neared and Operation Edzell was producing the evidence they needed. Time was now on their side.

Then disaster struck on the morning of 5 June, when the *Star* newspaper, the smallest of Britain's tabloids, carried a front-page story about Colin Stagg under the huge banner headline: 'I did not murder Rachel Nickell.' Mike Wickerson, Keith Pedder and Lizzie James were driving north to see Paul Britton when nature forced a call at a motorway service station. Pedder looked round in the car park as he got out of the car and saw the headlines in a copy of the *Star* being read by a man in a vehicle behind him. For a moment the officers couldn't believe their eyes. They took another look, then rushed off to buy their own copy of the *Star* in the nearest newsagent. Across the front and two inside pages was a full interview with the man who had occupied their attention for nearly ten months, saying he was innocent, that the police were trying to pin on him a murder he had not committed, that it was victimisation. Was this to be the end of an inquiry that was so tantalisingly close to solving Britain's foremost murder mystery?

To try to minimise the damage, Lizzie James went straight on the phone to Stagg. She lambasted him for getting involved with the press, professing to be upset at the damage it would do their relationship. Stagg seemed undeterred at the new blaze of publicity the story had brought him. Just ten days later, as the police were still wondering exactly what they should do in the circumstances, Stagg wrote Lizzie another sickening fantasy, so closely aligned to the Rachel murder that it was almost as if he was revelling in his notoriety. He said he and another, unnamed, male would be involved in a simulated rape with a tall, sexy blonde on Wimbledon Common. He would use a knife on the woman's vagina, bringing it round and cutting her during sexual intercourse 'mixing together the blood and semen and watching it splash over her genitalia and legs and those of the other man'. Stagg followed up with a phone call saying he wanted to act out the fantasy in real life as soon as possible.

It was decision time for the police — to carry on or pull Lizzie out. The next step, they knew, could place her in the greatest danger yet. They considered that Stagg was stoked up sexually and becoming more demanding by the day. How far should a young woman police officer be expected to go in the pursuit of justice? Fortunately for Lizzie, she never had to find out. Another high-level conference between the police, Paul Britton and the CPS decided that the covert operation should be disengaged. They decided that because of the *Star* story Stagg was now highly unlikely ever to confess to Lizzie that he was Rachel's killer. From an evidential point of view, they also feared that the publicity would probably encourage a ragtag assortment of deviants, cranks and weirdos to write to Stagg, thus greatly diminishing the value of the material so painstakingly gathered by Lizzie in the six months of Operation Edzell. It was another accurate prediction.

Lizzie James quickly cooled her relationship with Stagg, received a goodbye letter from him and went back to normal duties, her evidence amounting to a massive 1,700 pages in the police file. But was it enough? It was time for the Crown Prosecution Service to decide if Colin Stagg had a case to answer or whether Lizzie James had worked her dangerous mission in vain, leaving the Wimbledon murder team back at square one.

'I'm No Devil's Disciple'

Colin Stagg was in full flow as he sat on his tasselled settee, verbally lashing the police. In white shorts and black, short-sleeved T-shirt, he looked like a fresh-faced athlete taking a break from training. But Colin Stagg was talking about devil worship and pagan sacrifices and why he thought the police wanted to nail him for Rachel Nickell's murder. 'They think I did it because I believe in witchcraft,' he said. 'Just because I've got my bedroom painted black.'

Journalist Nick Constable had knocked on the door

of 16 Ibsley Gardens several times, keen for an in-depth interview with the man who bore such a striking resemblance to the *Crimewatch* videofit of the Rachel Nickell murder suspect. Not surprisingly the door had always been slammed in his face or had simply stayed closed. Constable, then working for the *Star*, was persistent. He felt that a man who had been grilled for three days by the police over the Rachel murder and who lived in a neat maisonette with 'Christians Keep Away: A Pagan Dwells Here' daubed on the door, must be worth talking to.

He was certainly surprised when the door was cautiously opened on the morning of 4 July. Constable introduced himself, said would like a chat about recent events, and Stagg said, 'Yeah, you'd better come in.' It was a couple of weeks from the anniversary of the murder and to the outside world the investigation had gone very cold. Stagg was surprisingly affable. 'The police were convinced it was me,' he told Constable. 'It was mainly because of my religion. I follow the Wicca religion, which was around before Christianity. People call it witchcraft nowadays but that gives the wrong impression. We believe all life is sacred I wouldn't hurt a spider. Yet when the police pulled me in last September they kept insisting I was practising Satanism and they tied that in with the murder of Rachel Nickell. They found some pigeon feathers on my windowsill and reckoned I'd been involved in some sort of ritual sacrifice. In fact pigeons just sat there and shed a few feathers. I've heard of rituals taking place on the common but I've never got involved. I follow my religion in my own home, my own way.'

Indeed, the whole maisonette bore evidence of his intense interest in paganism and the occult. The black bedroom walls were adorned with ancient symbols dating back to Saxon times — a stag to represent hunting and fertility, the famous Cerne Abbas giant with penis erect, a figure of a horned and masked creature. The elongated Uffington horse hovered above his bed, nearby was written the word Thunor, Anglo-Saxon for Thor; the Norse god of thunder. A variety of other occult symbols made up the rest of an extraordinary pastiche. Knives, swords and shields adorned the walls, a crossbow and bolts lay on the bedroom table. Dominating the bizarre scene was an altar adorned with Saxon shields and sword blades, plus a wooden dowsing stick.

Only weeks after Rachel's murder secret police video cameras had filmed weird rituals taking place in the moonlight on Wimbledon Common at the spot where Rachel died. The cameras captured a woman and two men performing what appeared to be some sort of black magic dance. All three were high on drugs. They were subsequently traced by the police and eliminated from the murder inquiry. Stagg had no connection with any of them.

Stagg told Constable that he had been left in no doubt that he was the prime suspect for the killing after his arrest and detention the previous September; when four separate callers from the Alton Estate named him as looking like the *Crimewatch* videofit.

'The police would play silly games with me,' he said. 'The first night I was in the cell they kept calling out my name to wake me up or offering me a drink of water when I'd never asked for one. It didn't bother me. I couldn't sleep so I was up reading a book. During the interviews they kept saying to me, "Why did you do it? Why did you murder her?" I kept telling them I hadn't even seen her. But I knew I was sure to be questioned as soon as I heard about it, but I'd got nothing to hide. I'm always up on the common with my dog Brandy. I never go anywhere without him. But I was there at 9:15 a.m. and then went home with a headache and slept. It wasn't the fact that I was questioned about the murder that bothered me. I knew the police were only doing their duty. What really annoyed me was the fact that people in the nearby flats were spreading lies about me. They said that I would pester and annoy women and that I was a pervert.'

He delivered his protest with the conviction of a man seemingly airing a genuine grievance, a protestation of wounded innocence.

On the mantelpiece, in pride of place, was a photograph of a young lady who, at that moment in time, had good cause to believe he was anything but innocent — his 'girlfriend' Lizzie James. It meant little at the time to Nick Constable. He knew nothing about the secret police operation that was going on. His trained eye scanned the well-kept maisonette and was intrigued at the paraphernalia, the strange aura of another belief from another part of time.

He'd got a good interview and was happy that he'd be on the front page with his story next morning. As he rose to leave he noted Stagg's reading material on the bookshelves, including titles like *Cult and Occult*, *Afterlife*, *Earth Mysteries* and *Sixth Sense*. A young man truly immersed in his beliefs, he thought, as Stagg posed for photographer Tony Sapiano in the back garden, affectionately scratching the ear of mongrel Brandy. As the reporter was leaving Stagg added, 'The police still hassle me, you know. They stop me near the common and say "Hello, Colin, have you got something you want to tell us?" I ask them, "What have you got in mind?" '

Constable had no idea of the furore his story would cause among the police team when it hit the streets the following day. After all, he had lunched with John Bassett a couple of weeks earlier and had explained that he was trying to get an interview with Colin Stagg. Bassett, he said, had given no indication that it might cause a problem. Constable, now working as a freelance in his native West Country after voluntarily leaving the *Star* for a green-field lifestyle, said, 'As far as I was concerned this was a perfectly valid journalistic exercise and I didn't feel obliged to tell the police in advance that we were going to publish the story. Mr Bassett knew I was trying to talk to Stagg and if it posed a problem to the investigation he should have indicated that fact to me at the time. It could quite easily have been done without divulging details of the secret operation that was going on with the policewoman. I'm sure the *Star* would not have run the story if there was any suggestion that it might prejudice the police inquiry.'

The police, by this time, had made extensive inquiries of their own about the Wicca religion in which Stagg so openly confessed his involvement. Could it be significant in the Rachel murder? Was it really black magic under another name? Some sort of devil worship? They sought the academic opinion of leading authorities in ancient cults and religions in an attempt to define the teachings of Wicca. It was, the detectives learned, a religion based on the love of nature, the sun, the moon and the seasons. There were witches and wizards with supernatural powers and magical rites in woodland glades — all seemingly innocent stuff by modern-day standards. But deep in the history of the cult there was also evidence of human sacrifice. In parts of Brittany, centuries ago, massive wicker baskets would be filled with potential victims for sacrificial slaughter; often criminals or other undesirables. They would be hauled from the wicker cage and set alight in front of chanting crowds as an appeasement to the nature spirits.

In 1973 the religion was featured in a film called *The Wicker Man*, starring Edward Woodward, Britt Ekland and horror star Christopher Lee. Woodward, television's *Equaliser* and presenter of *In Suspicious Circumstances*, played a detective lured to a Scottish island to investigate the disappearance of a schoolgirl. He unearths a terrifying world of sexual deviants, devil worship and pagan rituals. He is eventually burned alive inside a huge figure of a man woven out of wicker.

Today's followers of Wicca, the police discovered, could be numbered in thousands, ranging from the genuinely fascinated to the disillusioned and sometimes disgusting. The Pagan Federation, anxious that its image is projected sympathetically, had produced a useful booklet for those interested in unravelling the mysteries of this alternative creed. The important date in the pagan calender is Halloween, the old Celtic feast of Samhain, signifying the death of the old year and the birth of the new: the time when the gates between this world and the next are opened. For covens in Britain, this is a time to form a ritual circle around the altar and invite the spirits of the past to join them. A pagan altar symbolises the battle between good and evil. Joss sticks, candles, a container of salt and one of Glastonbury water symbolise the four elements of air, fire, earth and water. White and black cords represent light and dark. Flowers and candles are always brought from right to left to bring light into darkness. Pagans are emphatic that they do not recognise Satan — the devil, they say, is a Christian invention. Their god is Pan, the small, horned figure often featured on a pagan altar and a pre-Christian symbol of the fertility of the earth. Leading practitioners of Wicca are trying to establish their own recognised church in England, with legal rights of service and protection under the laws of blasphemy.

The foremost authority on Wicca in Britain, Michael York, a PhD from the Academy for Cultural and Education Studies in London, was able to provide the most authoritative assessment, based on more than 200 hours' participation and involvement in the religion, talking to leading members and watching ancient rituals. Though not a practitioner of Wicca himself, he told the police he found it a 'cogent and ethical' faith. Dr York had delivered important presentations on neo-paganism in Britain, America and France and was a trusted confidant of most leading Wiccan figures throughout Europe and the USA. He was the man, police realised, who really knew his stuff in this Wicca's world and his fourteen-page report was regarded as the most definitive they could expect to find on this somewhat rarefied subject. Dr York wrote,

> 'The Wiccan religion takes many forms, but its central features include a focus upon the female metaphor for the Godhead (usually designated the Goddess), a regard for the sacredness of nature and belief in the inherent or potential divinity of every human being. A masculine image of the Godhead is sometimes included (referred to as the God) and is recognised in such configurations as Herne the Hunter or the Green Man of British folklore tradition. But because of the virtual elimination of the feminine element in the Christian expression of Western culture, Wiccans tend to stress their understanding of, and concern with, their female configuration for divinity. This last is seen as comprising all the various forces of nature, the physical embodiment of the world and the spiritual reality to be found behind the phenomenal or natural world. This ubiquity of divinity in all beings leads to the Wiccan assertion that every human being is inherently divine. This in turn leads to the Wiccan affirmation that each individual is responsible for his or her own actions.'

This was, of course, precisely what Stagg was saying, in less academic terms, about his beliefs and assertions. The Archdeacon of Durham, Michael Perry, writes in his book *Gods Within, a Critical Guide to the New Age*, 'Wicca is a gentle religion'. It is practised alone, in small groups called covens, or larger groups called groves. 'The rites and gatherings of Wicca are timed in general to the phases of the moon,' said Dr York,

'. . . and to a calendar of seasonal festivals in which the changes of the agrarian year are seen as parallels to the human and inner spiritual development of the individual. The essential Wiccan ceremony consists of invoking the Goddess by magical practice within the confines of a sacred circle created for the occasion. The objective of Goddess invocation and the accompanying ceremony is to bring about inner transformation, the helping of others, or the healing of the earth. To my knowledge, both through first-hand observation and through reports of other academics and clergymen, Wicca never seeks to harm others or to practise so-called "black magic" . . . In my opinion there is nothing insidious or malevolent in the practice or expression of this particular nature-based religion, which respects the individual, the interaction of all life, and the healing processes which are seen as nature's balance.'

Dr York quotes another expert, the Rev. Lowell Streiker; as saying,

> 'The fundamental problem faced by "The Crafte" is the bad press it has suffered for several centuries. The public confuses gentle practitioners of simple magic with creatures of popular mythology who reject God and orthodox doctrine, worship Satan and sign their souls over to him, sacrifice animals and infants, engage in orgies and fly through the air on broomsticks. The failure to distinguish between (a) the "old religion", in which simple rituals are employed to assure good crops, healthy livestock, fertile families, good health, prosperity, freedom from stress and general wellbeing, and (b) the almost entirely fictional entity portrayed as witchcraft in the movies, theatre, tabloids and television, is wrong and unjust.'

It was a fascinating but intangible avenue of inquiry which the detectives felt somehow had a greater bearing on the investigation than was apparent at that moment. It was clearly an important part of their chief suspect's lifestyle but whether it was compensation for a life unfulfilled, or something more sinister; they did not know. If it was a sincerely held belief, they felt, he was hardly likely to have advertised his involvement with crude slogans daubed on his front door for all to see. If it was more sinister, the same would apply.

It was curious that one of the senior investigating

officers in the case was called Wickerson — a son of Wicker? The gritty detective, ex-drug squad with six previous murder inquiries to his credit, was happy that there were no mystical roots to his family tree that would give him anything more than a professional interest in this mysterious world.

Stagg, not a great socialiser but nevertheless a familiar figure on the Alton Estate, was getting a hard time from some people but he was still welcome in a few homes, including that of near neighbour Tina Burridge. He popped in two or three times a week for a chat and a cup of coffee. Like everyone else, Tina knew that he'd been questioned about Rachel Nickell, then released. She took the charitable view that if he hadn't been charged he must be presumed innocent. She and Stagg mentioned the Nickell case occasionally in their chats, with Stagg always maintaining that he was innocent. 'He wouldn't go into detail but said he didn't have anything to do with it,' she said. He also announced proudly to Tina that he'd got a girlfriend called Lizzie, that he was very fond of her and that he hoped she was going to come and stay at his home. He spoke dreamily of her getting time off from her job at a cattery in Slough and visiting him in Roehampton in the near future. Lizzie, he told Tina, was a pretty divorcee who had been involved in a Satanic relationship when she was younger. And, he confided, she was a bit kinky and wanted him to tie her up and abuse her. Out of casual curiosity Tina asked if Stagg was into that sort of thing. He told her initially that he didn't think he could do it but he later changed his tune and said that if Lizzie insisted he would have to 'give it a go'.

The conversation aroused no suspicions. They often talked freely on a variety of subjects. Tina had, after all, known all the Stagg boys, Colin, Tony, Lee and Peter; and their sister Julie ever since they were all at school together and had met Colin regularly on the common and around the estate when they walked their dogs together. Her dogs, a boxer and an alsatian, got on well with Stagg's Brandy and Colin had been able to show her lots of interesting new walks on the common that she never even knew existed. One thing was for sure, Stagg knew Wimbledon Common like the back of his hand — equally as well as the urban foxes that roamed its acres and whose tracks and earths Stagg pointed out with the enthusiasm of a nature rambler.

Tina also regarded Stagg as brighter than average — she knew he had passed an entry exam for the RAF when he was nineteen but had been unable to enlist because of a medical problem — and he had confessed the most personal of secrets to her just a few months earlier: he was a virgin. He had never; he said during one of their more intimate chats, had sexual intercourse with a girl. Tina got the impression that Stagg was desperate to lose his virginity and hoped that his new girlfriend Lizzie would be the one to help him to achieve his desire.

What he didn't mention was that, in the meantime, he was not averse to going on to the common for a bit of gay sex to satisfy his lust. It wasn't difficult to find a partner in the park virtually any day of the week. One gay man had already told police that he became scared when he took a stroll with a man who looked like Stagg near one of the ponds. This man, he said, had taken him to a remote pathway and his attitude had frightened him. That was enough to send the man on a hasty retreat and made him feel so concerned that he felt obliged to file a report at Wimbledon police station.

Stagg never tried on anything of a sexual nature with Tina, never showed any violence — just the occasional display of bad temper — and she had no cause to fear him or to believe that he was capable of hurting anyone, let alone killing someone in cold blood in front of a baby boy. However, when the videofit of the suspected killer had come on the television she had had to admit that it looked a lot like Colin Stagg. It left her wondering about the boy next door who'd so often escorted her across Wimbledon Common.

To the outside world the Nickell inquiry seemed, after twelve months, to have almost ground to a halt. An astonishing number of suspects — over 30 to date — had been arrested, questioned and released. Nobody could remember a modern-day murder inquiry in which so many men had been hauled in. But because of its emotional implications, this investigation had generated far more information than other cases. The police computers held nearly 7,000 files on possible suspects, known sex offenders, witnesses and various sources of information. Two of the suspects — since eliminated — had made headline news. One was Ben Silcock, a 27-year-old schizophrenic who was mauled by a lion at London Zoo on New Year's Eve 1992, after climbing into its cage to feed it chicken meat. As Silcock lay in intensive care after the tragedy, it emerged that he had been questioned in connection with Rachel's murder after police were told he regularly roamed Wimbledon

Common. Silcock, who also lived in Roehampton, and was said to have an obsession with cats large and small, was quickly eliminated. However; his case helped to highlight the problems of schizophrenics in society and brought a pledge from the government of greater care in the future.

The other suspect was dashing ex-soldier Roderick Newall, who was later involved in a dramatic arrest on the high seas off Gibraltar. At the time he was being sought by police in the Channel Islands in connection with the murders of his parents. The Royal Naval frigate *Argonaut* was used to intercept Newall as he sailed his luxury yacht in the Atlantic, 150 miles south west of Gibraltar. When he was successfully detained and taken to the Rock to await questioning, police at Wimbledon confirmed that he was also on their computer list of suspects for the Rachel Nickell murder. They had discovered that Newall had been staying with friends in Mortlake, just a few miles from Wimbledon Common, at the time of the murder and had disappeared in a hurry immediately afterwards. Newall was subsequently cleared by the police of any involvement in Rachel's murder but then charged with murdering his parents for inheritance money. (His brother; Mark, was charged with helping to dispose of their bodies. Both are now in jail).

Four months after the murder, two detectives from the Wimbledon incident office flew to Italy to interview a gravedigger who had disappeared on 16 July, 24 hours after the killing. Henry Lavelle, aged 28, worked at Putney Vale Cemetery, adjoining Wimbledon Common. A police tracker dog had followed the scent of the murder suspect from the murder scene into the massive graveyard. Mrs Marjorie Piper, who had been visiting the cemetery on the morning of the murder, had told detectives how she had heard someone running quickly on the other side of the fence. 'It was like someone running through trees,' she said. She couldn't see anyone and the mystery footsteps quickly faded. She thought nothing of it until she heard of the murder; then realised it might have been the killer fleeing. Officers who questioned twenty other graveyard workers were told that Mr Lavelle had travelled to Europe the next day to look for a job in a vineyard. The police decided that because of his proximity to the murder he must be interviewed personally by officers from the Wimbledon team. He was traced through Interpol and two officers flew to Treviso, sixteen miles north of Venice, to interview him at the offices of the British Consulate. However, his trip to Italy was perfectly innocent and he, too, was swiftly eliminated from further inquiries.

Photography student Simon Murrell was arrested in a massive blaze of publicity — the thirteenth suspect to be taken in for questioning. He had been named as the possible killer in a tipoff to a Sunday newspaper. He was seized at his home in the Toxteth area of Liverpool and faced a jeering 200-strong mob as he left a Merseyside police station to be driven to Wimbledon. He, too, was quickly eliminated from inquiries but by then he was front-page news and his life had been delved into by dozens of reporters. His lawyer, Robert Broudie, was furious. 'There is something seriously wrong with police procedure,' he complained, 'when an innocent man who is held for questioning can be held up to public vilification this way. It has been a gross slur on his character and has put a huge strain on him and his family. The whole affair has been an enormous shock to him.' The incident provoked a rash of apologies to Mr Murrell in the press and raised again the rights and wrongs, advantages and drawbacks of the great publicity machine in cases which generate such passion. Publicity can so often assist in major police inquiries and is actively sought by forces throughout the country. By the same token, it can devastate the lives of those hit by the fall-out when the wrong target is struck.

The Nickell investigation illustrated, too, the high price of a murder investigation in Britain today. As costs soared towards one and a half million, Scotland Yard was already providing additional cash from central budgeting to assist the local force. Never for a moment did the police consider winding it down completely. They might have to reduce the number of officers employed on the inquiry but the file would always be open while the killer was still on the loose. The British police have a satisfying clear up rate for murder — they solve about 90 per cent of the 600 to 700 murders a year. Many, particularly domestic killings, are quickly dealt with, tying up just a handful of officers for a few days. Those like the apparently random murder of Rachel Nickell can easily stretch to months or even years. In such a high-profile murder, public expectations of an arrest and conviction are high. No-one at Wimbledon police station was about to give up on Rachel Nickell. When Scotland Yard's accountants ordered Detective Superintendent Bassett to keep the overtime payments under control his men said, 'Don't worry, Guv, we'll do it without extra pay.'

Many officers were carrying out far more than the recommended number of inquiries under police guidelines, ten times the workload in some cases, but no-one was complaining.

Bassett — affectionately known as Bertie Bassett to his loyal team — was by now nearing the end of a long and successful career in the police force. He didn't want to clear his desk with the Rachel Nickell file stamped 'UNSOLVED'. It was probably his most awesome job in 30 years of police work. He knew the Lizzie James operation had hit trouble but he was not the sort of man to talk defeat. There was a touch of Inspector Morse about Bassett — quiet, intelligent, private and compassionate. His marriage ended during the Rachel Nickell inquiry but he never said why or whether it was connected with the pressures. He retained a friendly, easy-going manner. On the first day of the inquiry, as news was emerging of just how ghastly a murder it was, he appeared to be smiling as he gave interviews for newspaper and television journalists in Windmill Road, just on the edge of Wimbledon Common. It seemed at odds with the gravity of the situation but, in fact, he wasn't smiling at all, it was a nervous reaction to the emotional strains of the day which turned the corners of his mouth upwards in an avuncular expression. John Bassett felt anger and sorrow for Rachel and her little boy as much as anyone. He recalled, 'That first morning . . . thank God I haven't come across scenes like that too often. I was horrified when I saw Rachel lying there and the little boy, caked in his mother's blood, sitting shocked in the back of a police van. But personal feelings do not solve murders. That is a dry, detailed, exacting process. Nothing like the way you see it on the TV or films.'

Born in Orpington, Kent, where his father had a small haulage business, Bassett joined the police force in 1960 and worked his way up to the top level of CID investigators with a reputation for shrewd judgement and a gritty thoroughness. His relaxations away from the job were golf, flying and travel. He became interested in the relatively new concept of offender profiling when he led the investigation into the kidnap of baby Alexandra Griffiths from St Thomas's Hospital in south London. He became convinced that the kidnapper had some personal connection with the hospital, rather than being someone who had just walked in off the street and snatched the baby. Sure enough, when the baby was found in Burford, Oxfordshire, seventeen days later; after a tip-off to *The Sun*, the woman kidnapper turned out to be a former outpatient who had acquired bogus nursing qualifications and was obsessed with getting a baby of her own, just as the experts had predicted. Bassett was equally convinced now that the combined expertise of Britton and Ressler held the key to solving Rachel's murder. He knew, thanks to them, just what sort of man he was looking for and he was acutely aware of Paul Britton's chilling prediction that killers in this mould often strike again just a year later. Now the twelve months were up. He studied the file on Colin Stagg once again. He knew that soon he would have to make the most important decision of his career — to order the arrest of Stagg on a charge of murder; or to tell Andrew and Monica Nickell that he was sorry but there was just not enough evidence and it was time to wind the investigation down. The grey-haired policeman on his last big case said philosophically, 'I'm here to take the accolades if we are successful, so I am here to take the brickbats if we fail.'

For months after the murder, Mike Wickerson got in his car once a week and drove to Wimbledon Common, parking up near the old Windmill. He walked from the car park to the spot where Rachel died, looking, hoping for inspiration. Sometimes he stood silently watching the stream of men who came and went, wondering if one of them was the killer who had vanished into nowhere. Now Colin Stagg, a man who prowled that common more than anyone, preoccupied his mind. He was pretty sure, by now, what Stagg was all about.

It was, by any yardstick, a difficult and frustrating murder inquiry. What the police team needed least of all were the weirdos who, for whatever pitiful reason, chose to supply false leads, lure detectives up blind alleys and waste huge amounts of time and money. The Wimbledon squad had their fair share but none was more convincing or contrived than Susan Jacqueline Eyles, who played two separate roles in an attempt to persuade the police that she knew the identity of Rachel's killer. She first phoned the police, giving her name as Helen, and saying that an acquaintance called Gary Edmondson had confessed to the killing. He had allegedly said he didn't mean to murder her but just wanted sex and was 'freaked out' when the little boy screamed. Helen said she thought Gary had someone else with him, another man, at the time. So convincing was her story that detectives had every reason to believe her call was genuine and that it was a lead to be given the highest priority. For another month Helen made numerous other calls to the murder squad but failed to deliver the vital information which would lead them to the suspect Gary. Asked why she was holding back, she told them, in apparent embarrassment, that she was having a sexual relationship with a cousin and was frightened of being arrested herself if the police quizzed her. She said she had also been threatened by the second man allegedly involved in attacking Rachel because she was asking too many questions. She said she feared for her safety if the two men got to know she was talking to the police.

At the end of October 1992, she finally told the police that Gary was hiding out at an address in Manchester. A team of officers immediately drove north to check out the information. The man Edmondson was not at the house but police still believed Helen was genuine because she had given the correct phone number at the address and had correctly identified one of the other occupants. It still looked like a live lead.

Then a fortnight later, an American-sounding woman, calling herself Josie, called police to say she was worried about another girl living in the same house, who was somehow linked to the Rachel Nickell inquiry. Josie, who said she was a student, claimed the other woman, whom she named as Helen, had told her she knew who had murdered Rachel. It looked, on the surface, like further confirmation of the 'Gary Edmondson' lead. Josie phoned several times for another two weeks, giving more and more detail about Helen and Gary, but she failed to produce enough concrete evidence for the police to move in and make an arrest. She used the old excuse that she 'didn't want to get involved'. The police were beginning to get suspicious but, as the inquiry was already heavily underway, it was decided to carry on with inquiries.

Extensive inquiries were made through criminal records and police intelligence networks in a bid to trace all, or any, of the three people involved to date: Helen, Josie or Gary. In an attempt to find Josie, police checked at universities where American students might be studying, as well as at the US embassy and the University of California, from which Josie was thought to have transferred to a college in England. To try to trace Gary Edmondson, detectives searched the National Registration of births, marriages and deaths at St Catherine's House and pored over hundreds of voters' lists in the Southfields area of West London where he was supposed to live. Every avenue of inquiry drew a blank so the police called in British Telecom experts to trace any further calls from either Helen or Josie. The next call from Helen was quickly pinpointed to Cheltenham in Gloucestershire. It was made from a firm called the Cheltenham Induction Heating Company in the town's Saxon Way. The next call was traced to a telephone kiosk nearby. Police decided to run checks on all five women employed by the heating firm, drove down to the West Country on 24 November nearly two months after the first call had triggered off the inquiry, and confronted Susan Eyles. She admitted she was the bogus Helen.

Eventually, under tape-recorded interrogation, she confessed that she had, in fact, concocted the whole thing, that she hadn't been under any pressure from anyone, and that she was suffering from a problem she didn't want to discuss with the police officers.

She was charged with wasting police time, put on probation for a year; and recommended to seek psychiatric help. Her absurd invention had cost the police almost £6,000 and tied up murder squad officers for many hours on a wild-goose chase when they could have been used on genuine lines of inquiry. Nobody knew quite why she did it. Unfortunately, in almost every major police inquiry — as was illustrated in the case of kidnapped baby Abbie Humphries in Nottingham — there will always be some twisted souls who seek to complicate the most delicate of police investigations.

If any purpose could be served from Susan Eyles' unwelcome intrusion into the Rachel Nickell case it was to give the police ammunition to refute subsequent claims by defence lawyers that they had conducted the inquiry in a blinkered fashion once Colin Stagg had been accepted as the number-one suspect. How could this be possible, they argued, when so many suspects had been questioned, so many leads followed up in the relentless pursuit of the killer? They pointed out that the undercover operation involving Lizzie James was underway when Susan Eyles came on the scene and if they had excluded all suspects apart from Colin Stagg, as was alleged, they would not have chased her story with such enthusiasm, using so many and so varied a range of police resources.

The Wimbledon team were also to face defence accusations at an official level that they had deliberately leaked information to the press in an attempt to blacken Colin Stagg's name and expose him to unwarranted and damaging media attention. This, too, was vehemently denied. Their only concern, said the CID team, was to catch the killer fair and square, whoever he might be.

Arrest at Dawn

The decision to charge Colin Stagg with Rachel's murder was taken in August 1993, one year and one month after the nightmare attack. The evidence had been carefully analysed by the Crown Prosecution Service's most eminent criminal lawyers, acutely aware that facets of the inquiry were certain to be so highly contentious that the Nickell case was likely to find itself written into the law manuals. The police team at Wimbledon were told in the second week in August to bring Stagg in.

The prime suspect was still asleep when detectives rapped on his door in the half-light of dawn on 17 August 1993. He stumbled to the door, bleary-eyed, to be told that new evidence had come to light in the Rachel Nickell inquiry and that he was being arrested for murder. 'Who's been causing trouble?' he asked Keith Pedder. The police team swarmed into his home, armed with a search warrant, and began to take the place apart in a relentless quest for evidence. 'Is it someone round here?' he demanded to know. 'I didn't do it. Someone is causing trouble.'

Pedder was accompanied by Martin Long, the officer who had assisted him so well in the long hours of interviewing when Stagg had been arrested the first time round, over a year ago now. Detective Constable Long had left the Wimbledon squad as the numbers were gradually wound down and had gone back to the Regional Crime Squad office in Surbiton, Surrey, back into the world of 'blaggers', drug dealers and stolen-car rackets, but with Colin Francis Stagg never very far from his thoughts. When Pedder got the go-ahead to re-arrest Stagg, he phoned Long and told him, 'I want you back here, Martin. This could be it.' It was the news Martin Long had been waiting for; a conclusion to the Rachel Nickell case at last, he hoped.

The Alton Estate was now coming to life, with faces peering through curtains as Stagg was driven off to Wimbledon police station for the second time in the investigation. He refused to answer questions about the murder, as was his right in law. As he was charged and cautioned, he told the police: 'I'm bloody innocent. I've been stitched up with this. Now I'm going to lose my home and my dog. The man who did this is laughing at you.'

In the circumstances, it was extraordinary that a man facing the possibility of life imprisonment for the most shocking murder in Britain for years should be worrying about his dog. He insisted that it went back to Rita Nagy to be cared for before he would consent to leave the maisonette and go to the police station. In fact, Brandy was sent to pleasant kennels in Windsor.

Blue-overalled police officers, carrying spades, forks, trowels and a metal detector; began a systematic sweep of Stagg's back garden. They dug and delved, poked and prodded all day, looking for any items which might have been buried and for traces of ashes which might indicate some recently burned items like shoes or clothing. The garden was dug to a depth of two feet and fuchsias, irises and Japanese anemones were carefully lifted and replaced. Some were even given a good watering before they were restored to the soil to carry on blooming in peace. A compost bin was emptied and searched, pots containing patio shrubs were checked for hidden contents. What the police hoped for was a rusting, single-edged sheath knife buried somewhere on the plot — a knife which bore similarities to the murder weapon which had been so carefully reconstructed by Dr Shepherd from his examination of Rachel's wounds. It was not to be. The garden yielded no significant clues.

Inside the maisonette other officers examined every drawer; cupboard, cavity and crevice, probed the mattress and looked under the floorboards. Most of Stagg's clothing and items thought relevant to the inquiry were taken away in brown sacks to be examined forensically. With what the police now knew of Stagg's sexual inclinations, they would not have been surprised to have discovered a hoard of sordid, sado-masochistic literature, but there were only two soft-porn magazines, available from the top shelf at almost any newsagents, tucked away in the bedroom, and a few full-frontal pin-up photos of women stuck on the walls of the room he used as a gymnasium. It was the kind of material that would not have been unusual for any bachelor to have in his home. What was more interesting to the police was a series of sexy letters from a woman in Wales, which had been sent to Stagg after the *Star* story was published in July — just the sort of thing they had feared might happen as they terminated the Lizzie James operation. This, they realised, was someone switched on to Stagg's sordid wavelength. Rather than watering down the quality of Lizzie's evidence, however; what they now had was a genuine devotee of the pain and pleasure world of sado-masochism, who might even add support to the police case. Two officers were despatched to Swansea to interview Janet George and recover any letters she might have received from Colin Stagg. They found seven and a series of photographs of Stagg.

Janet George was a reluctant witness from the outset, terrified that her secret shame was about to become public knowledge. Yes, she said, she had written highly explicit letters to Stagg, and no, she was not offended by anything he had written back to her. She said she had let her imagination 'run wild' in creating sexual fantasies to send to him. It was one of those odd phenomena that defy explanation: a rather plain woman from a backstreet in Wales writing out of the blue to a man she knew was suspected of committing a demented murder in front of a little boy. What was the macabre bond which drew such people together, the police wondered. This attraction to notoriety was not that unusual either, which was why they had felt forced to abandon the Lizzie operation before it became tarnished by the attentions of other oddballs. Convicted criminals and those suspected of major crimes have attracted a lurid 'fan mail' the world over, with the likes of Yorkshire Ripper Peter Sutcliffe and America's Jeffrey Dahmer receiving many unsolicited approaches from the curious, the crazy and the quick-buck brigade out to sell inside information to the media. Janet George was not a happy woman as police told her she could become a witness for the Crown in an Old Bailey trial certain to attract major publicity.

Stagg's arrest, the culmination of thirteen months' hard work and a certain amount of table thumping by Keith Pedder at the CPS offices, was cause for a minor celebration at murder headquarters — until the national papers arrived next morning. Once more police and press were in conflict. *The Sun* and the *Mirror* had both revealed details of the undercover police operation involving Lizzie James. Other nationals picked up the line and it was in almost every tabloid on the morning of 19 August as Stagg prepared to make his first appearance in court on the murder charge. This was something the police had desperately wanted to keep under wraps. It was evidential — and, technically, the press should not publish any details of evidence once a suspect has been charged. More importantly, the police team and the CPS knew the Lizzie operation would certainly be vehemently objected to by defence lawyers very early in the legal proceedings and might even be ruled as inadmissible at the committal proceedings when a magistrate would be asked to decide whether or not there was a *prima facie* case to answer. They did not want potential Old Bailey jurors to be aware of the Lizzie involvement in case it was never presented as part of the police evidence. Jurors might read about it now and say, 'Well, where is it?' when the case came up for trial. They would wonder what had happened to such an important slice of prosecution evidence. It was an understandable concern — but equally understandable was the desire of the papers to use such an interesting angle on such an important story. It was a decision for newspaper lawyers and editors. Not many would have spiked it, knowing that a rival might well splash it across the front page next morning. The prickly question arose yet again of whether it is the job of newspapers to protect sensitive police investigations or to publish stories of undoubted interest to their readers once they are satisfied the information is accurate. With the requirements of police and press so frequently at variance, it is an argument that will probably never be concluded.

This time the animosity between press and police over the Nickell inquiry reached a new intensity. Scotland Yard's Complaints Investigation Branch were instructed to launch an inquiry to find out who had leaked the Lizzie story to the papers. Every officer on the inquiry with knowledge of the covert operation was questioned by the CIB in an attempt to identify the source of the leak. The Attorney General, Britain's senior law officer, issued writs against four daily newspapers, alleging contempt. To many of those on the newspaper side, it seemed to be an over-the-top kneejerk reaction but there was no mistaking the fury among police ranks. Mike Wickerson was understandably angry that the Rachel investigation might be in jeopardy. A story swept Fleet Street that he had threatened to take a swing at crime reporter Mike Sullivan, who he thought was the man from *The Sun* who had broken the Lizzie story — only to discover it was the wrong reporter. He was said to have grabbed the journalist by the lapels and told him in a furious eyeball-to-eyeball confrontation precisely what he thought of him. Like so much internal newspaper tittle tattle, however, the story appeared to have become somewhat exaggerated in the telling. The true version of events seemed to be that Wickerson, at the Old Bailey on matters unrelated to the Rachel Nickell inquiry, had bumped into a *Sun* reporter who was unconnected with the Stagg story and had lambasted him for his paper's alleged irresponsibility in running the line about Lizzie and the undercover operation. There was no threat of violence and the matter was resolved amicably over a pint at a nearby pub.

To the law and order authorities the Lizzie leak was clearly regarded as an important issue in that its eventual findings could well play a significant role in the continuing debate on threatened press curbs in Britain, and many man hours were to be invested in trying to trace the police 'mole' who had supposedly slipped such sensitive information to the papers. The journalists involved maintained that they were just doing the job they were paid to do — get stories.

As ever Andrew and Monica Nickell made a

dignified and reasoned response to Stagg's arrest. At home in Ampthill Mr Nickell said, 'We have always been optimistic that someone would be found for Rachel's death. The only thing that we would want is that this time the police will have clear evidence that someone was guilty. My wife and I believe in the English system of justice and we hope the person who is arrested has a fair trial. And if he is found guilty we hope the judge will make an appropriate sentence which, as far as we are concerned, is that he should stay in prison for the rest of his life.'

Colin Stagg appeared in court at Wimbledon on 18 August, looking unshaven from his dawn arrest the previous day and wearing a scruffy black T-shirt and blue jeans. He bit his lip nervously as the charge was read . . . 'that you did, on July 15 1992, murder Rachel Nickell on Wimbledon Common'. He was not invited to tender a plea at this early stage and, after a brief hearing during which he was flanked by two police officers, he was remanded in custody for 28 days and taken to Wandsworth Prison. Outside the court an angry crowd had gathered to see him leave but he was kept in the court cells for several hours and most people had drifted away by the time he eventually emerged in a prison van. The crowd had come from both the Alton Estate and the spacious grandeur of homes bordering the common to try to catch a glimpse of the man who had allegedly stamped notoriety on the pleasant suburb normally more famous for its lawn tennis and expensive strawberries. Some had armed themselves with eggs to throw in a sort of protest, a symbol of the anger the murder had generated, even though this was a man accused, not a man convicted. One of the onlookers, insurance broker's wife Diane Cornelius, dressed in an immaculate summer outfit, said, 'I came as a gesture of support to Rachel's family. They must be going through an awful time. I just wanted to show that the people of Wimbledon are thinking of them.'

Across Britain, the arrest had certainly rekindled memories of the smiling face of Rachel Nickell and her cruel fate on Wimbledon Common. It was progress at last in an inquiry that most people thought was firmly on the back burner. John Bassett had been at the back of the court for the Stagg hearing. He looked quietly confident. With three months to go before retirement, was this to be his finest hour? The police team were greatly encouraged by the fact that the prosecution was now being handled at the Crown Prosecution Service by a former policeman turned barrister named Bruce Butler. Here was a man who could look at the problems with the benefit of both legal and investigative expertise, a man prepared to listen and discuss.

Keith Pedder was a regular visitor to the CPS Tolworth Towers offices as he researched legal precedents which might help to guide the Stagg investigation through the dangerous waters ahead without allowing it to become wrecked on a legal rock. So frequently was the ex-public schoolboy — who admits to being expelled and 'having no choice but to join the police' — to be found with his head in a massive legal tome that he was often called 'Pedder QC' by his colleagues. This prosecution was personal to Keith Pedder and equally important for every pretty girl who might one day choose to walk on Wimbledon Common. His eighteen years' experience told him that whatever his police instincts dictated, he had to be right and this must not be a blinkered investigation. If Colin Stagg was his man he must be nailed by the book. With brilliant lawyer Bill Boyce appointed to lead the prosecution team in court the police now believed they had the A-team to present their case.

Andre Hanscombe had by now taken little Alex — four on 11 August — to a new home and a new life in France. The dream he and Rachel had nurtured together had come true, in part anyway, for father and son, with cherished memories now an enforced substitute for the golden girl, lover and mother, who had filled their lives with such joy. The scars were slowly healing, as much as was possible, but the call to Andre, telling him that Stagg had been arrested and charged, brought back all the memories of his abject despair when he learned of Rachel's death and how he had had to tell his son that Mummy wasn't coming home. He knew that he would probably have to relive his agony in public with Colin Stagg sitting just yards away in a court of law, accused of killing the girl he so loved and so missed. If he had needed strength in the past, he was certain to need it even more in the months to come.

Before moving to France, Andre had given an interview to *Hello!* magazine, telling how Alex was developing the same sunny disposition as his mother; despite the great trauma of her death. With the money from the *Hello!* and *Daily Mail* interviews, Andre planned to give his son a chance to escape the horrors of the past, to flee the dangers of London and build a secure life together in another place, in fresh air untainted by so many constant reminders. 'He only ever remembers his mother with a smile on her face,' said Andre.

'Wonderful people like Rachel leave part of themselves behind in everybody. It's staggering how normal he is now and that is a reflection of the time Rachel spent with him. She was with him all the time and we talked to him, even when he was in the womb. His personality is a lot like hers — sunny. He's only got me now and the most important thing is that he has as much of my attention as possible, because I can't bring her back for him. It's been a challenge figuring out what's for the best all the time. I was terrified at first that he would become a complete vegetable. The pressure was trying to do the right thing. When you've worked out what it is, it isn't hard. I miss talking to Rachel, but I don't find it hard making decisions without her because I'm convinced I know what her attitude would be to virtually everything. I knew her so well.'

Of the dangers of living in London, which had become so frighteningly obvious that summer day when Rachel died, he said:

'When you find out the kind of people who live in an area, how many past offenders, people out on bail, those let out after seventeen years, then you realise that every street, park or area is dangerous, night or day. You can't afford to let your children out of your sight, or let anybody vulnerable be in any situation on their own. It's totally unfair on women who are the victims and children who are at risk. Rachel was very much for equality and would shrug things off and say, "Don't be ridiculous. I can go and do what I want."

But one sexually depraved maniac had had different ideas that sunny July morning.

Stagg's mother, Hilda Carr, could never accept that her Colin could be that man, as the police were now claiming. Heaven knows, she had seen enough tragedy in the family without this, but Colin had never been a problem, even though they had seen virtually nothing of each other for almost twenty years after she had taken the decision to walk out on Vic. She had been surprised to get a letter from Colin soon after his court appearance for indecent exposure. It was the first since the family split up. Colin wrote from his Ibsley Gardens home: 'Mum, I'm just writing to you to give you reassurance that I am not a "pervert", the true story was, I was sunbathing nude over the common with my dog and apparently some woman saw me. Do not believe what you read in the newspapers, they've blown things out of proportion. So do not be ashamed of me. I am not a bloody deviant' — he heavily underlined the two final words. He sent all the best to his mother and added in a PS: 'This incident happened over two months ago (some time after that woman's murder) and the police wanted something [again underlined] on me.'

Hilda was devastated by the allegations against Colin. She had managed to cope somehow with Tony's rape conviction and with eldest son Lee's drug addiction, with the trauma of Lee's girlfriend jumping to her death from a tower block and daughter Julie's boyfriend being killed in a car crash, but this, the suggestion he had murdered Rachel Nickell, was too hard to bear and the family began to fear for her health. She wondered where it would end. Tony said, 'She told me that it was the end of the tether . . . if Colin was convicted she would kill herself'.

The nightmare seemed so far away from the day when Colin had been born on 20 May 1963 at King's Hospital, Chelsea, when the family was living in Humbolt Road, Hammersmith. With Vic in regular work as a billposter for an advertising agency, the family got by, but it all changed when Colin Stagg was five and Vic lost his job due to failing eyesight. They were forced to leave their tied house and move over the river to the Alton Estate. Vic was unable, or unwilling, to find other work and the marriage began to crack up. Colin was always a shy boy, squinting and clinging to his mother's hand as he was taken to the local Heathmere Primary School. He went on to the Elliot comprehensive, where classmates remembered him tearing up bibles as a pastime. Hilda decided to pack her bags when Colin was about twelve or thirteen. He never forgave her. Birthday cards and letters that she sent to him were ceremoniously torn up. Colin remained close to Vic Stagg and the two shared each other's company on walks on Wimbledon Common and when listening to records that Vic was happy to buy with his dole money. It triggered an interest in pop music and Colin had bought a guitar and learned to play a few chords — enough to get himself a slot in a group calling themselves The Filth. Their sole gig was believed to be a one-off date in a Fulham pub.

Vic Stagg suffered his first heart attack within a week of Hilda leaving. It only served to increase Colin's resentment. The last time he and his mother met, prior to his arrest, was at Vic Stagg's funeral in 1986. They didn't speak. 'It was a very tense occasion,' said aunt Patricia Young.

Colin's secondary-school career was punctuated with truancy and, despite an apparent flair for languages and art, he left with no 'O'-Levels. He became increasingly solitary, shy with girls and happy to be alone with his dog, his guitar and his paints, or playing heavy metal music plus Eric Clapton, the Eagles and R&B. After the death of his father he increasingly developed the passionate interest in Wicca and the occult which was to heap such suspicion upon him from the detectives looking for a motive and a suspect for Rachel Nickell's murder. He belonged to no accepted coven and one of the first questions police were asked by a leading 'high priestess' of Wicca was: is Stagg his real name or did he change it? The stag, she said, was among the most powerful of all the pagan symbols. It was indeed Colin Stagg's correct name, according to his birth certificate, said the detectives.

Time and time again the police went back to the report from Michael York, the witchcraft expert. The Wiccan god, identified with the Celtic king of the underworld, was a horned figure called Cernunnos, said

Dr York. Cernunnos was often called simply the Horned God and recognised in such folklore figures as the Green Man and Herne the Hunter. He was depicted on a Celtic cauldron discovered in Denmark, surrounded by animals, holding in his right hand a torque as a symbol of authority and in his left a serpent with a ram's head. The origins of Cernunnos are lost in the mists of time surrounding the hunting rituals of early palaeolithic man but the earliest representation of the god is probably in a rock carving at Val Camonicain in northern Italy, in which he is depicted as a tall, standing figure with antlers, torques and a serpent.

Dr York quotes expert Graham Webster, author of *The British Celts and Their Gods Under Rome*, as saying: 'Although the surviving evidence of horned deities in Britain is slight, it seems evident that it was widespread, even in the civil areas, and their power and significance far transcend any close association with hunting; they are part of the death and regeneration cycle.'

The legacy of the Horned God survives among some branches of Wicca in a recognition of Jack in the Green, the Green Man, Robin Hood and other similar figures of folklore and ecclesiastical ornamentation as the 'terrestrial aspect of the ancient Horned God of the Underworld', said Dr York. 'He is an earthly representation of cosmic harmony; of the geomantic equilibrium of solar and terrestrial forces . . . The Horned God and his Green Man aspect (all pagan personifications of the male principle within and behind visible creation) have been branded by Christians as the "devil" because, of course, the Green Man/Robin Hood and his followers were the Christians' greatest opponents — from the village priest to the distant archbishop.' Dr York quotes from Ian Taylor's book, *The Giant of Penhill*, where the author says the slaying of a boar by bow and arrow could have led to a somewhat confused account of a blood sacrifice — the use of the magical power of blood — to invoke the presence of the Green Man/Robin Hood'.

According to the book, *Folklore, Myths and Legends of Britain*, Michael York told the Wimbledon team, Herne the Hunter was a royal huntsman who saved a king's life by interposing his own body between a wounded stag and his master. As he lay mortally wounded, a wizard appeared and told the king that the only way to save Herne's life was to cut off the stag's antlers and tie them on to the huntsman's head. Herne recovered and, for years to come, enjoyed the king's favour. Then the other huntsmen, jealous of his influence, persuaded the king to dismiss him. Herne hanged himself and has haunted Windsor Great Park ever since. The stag's antlers almost certainly identify Herne as Cernunnos, God of the Underworld, who was once worshipped in the park and who, according to legend, still guards its ancient shrine and forest. He is most often seen during times of national crisis, near the site of a great oak which once grew in the park. He is said to have last been seen in 1962 when a group of youths found a hunting horn in the park and sounded it . . . Herne appeared riding a black steed, wearing chains on his body and with a stag's antlers growing from his brow.

These were ordinary coppers, trying to find a murderer and not at all sure quite where all this was leading. Was it crucial, or claptrap? These were implications the detectives were now being forced to consider.

In the Dock

An extraordinary division of loyalties developed on the Alton Estate in the months after Stagg's arrest. While many people who knew Stagg thought he was the killer, a growing number were becoming increasingly certain he was the innocent victim of a police 'fit-up'. His supporters, including his mother and stepfather and his legal representatives, argued that evidence had been tailored to fit Stagg and that offender profiles had been drawn up specifically with him in mind and in collusion with expert witnesses like Paul Britton and Dr Shepherd the pathologist.

Stagg's lawyers opted to put their case to the test by asking for a full old-style committal hearing at which the prosecution evidence could be fully exposed and challenged before a magistrate was asked to make a decision on whether Stagg should face trial at the Central Criminal Court, known more familiarly as the Old Bailey. Nowadays, most major cases are sent for trial on the submission of written evidence, but Stagg's legal team wanted the principal prosecution witnesses in court, live, so that they could face cross-examination, particularly key witnesses like Paul Britton and Lizzie James who represented the very cornerstone of the prosecution case. Defence barrister Jim Sturman intended to submit that their evidence was inadmissible and, if he won the point, would ask the magistrate to rule that there was no case to answer and ask that Colin Stagg should be freed immediately.

The committal hearing was to be taken by stipendiary magistrate Terry English, transferred specially from Camberwell Green Court in south London to hear the case at Wimbledon's brand-new courthouse just round the corner from the railway station. He was respected in the legal profession as an impartial and experienced adjudicator. As an outsider, a trained lawyer and a full-time magistrate hearing literally hundreds of cases a year, there could never be any suggestion of bias on his side.

Stagg was escorted into the dock of Wimbledon Magistrates' Court by a prison officer on the morning of 17 February 1994, his appearance so dramatically changed from the pictures shown of him in the newspapers the previous autumn that he could have been a different person. The close-cropped, curly hairstyle had given way to a longer, schoolboyish cut with a small quiff lobbing over his forehead. He appeared to have lost at least three stone in weight. He looked tiny and insignificant as all eyes focused on him. His mum and stepdad David Carr, in a smart Merchant Navy blazer, nodded at him reassuringly from the public seats. Nearby sat Stagg's new girlfriend, Diane Rooney, a busty blonde in her twenties with what appeared to be tiny tattoos on her slightly flushed cheeks. She had apparently befriended Stagg after his arrest and was a regular visitor to him in his remand cell at Wandsworth Prison in south London. Several residents from the Alton Estate crowded into the public gallery, some equipped with notebooks and pens, some loudly protesting Stagg's innocence in what seemed an almost orchestrated campaign, some simply curious about the man who had lived among them for so long and was now accused of such a dreadful murder.

The magistrate ruled that the proceedings should not be reported by the press, other than the basic details permitted by law — name, age, address and the charge faced — and that no photographs of Stagg should appear in newspapers or on television during the hearing or prior to his trial. In English magistrates' courts only, a defendant has the right to ask for reporting restrictions to be lifted — an option rarely exercised unless defence lawyers believe publicity would be an advantage. Stagg's legal team were adamantly against any such widespread exposure at this stage, fearing it might fan the flames of prejudice which they maintained were already surrounding certain aspects of the case. Jim Sturman pointed out that press publicity had already resulted in four daily newspapers being prosecuted for contempt over previously published stories about Stagg and, in view of the crucial issues of identity involved, asked that no photographs of him should appear in the papers or on TV at any time prior to the conclusion of all criminal proceedings. It was not an unreasonable request in the circumstances and it was pretty much a formality that Mr English would accede to it.

Stagg, in a grey sweatshirt with a black collar, looked intently at prosecutor William Boyce, flanked by seven manuals of evidence containing the statements of two dozen witnesses, as he outlined Rachel's final hours on the morning of 15 July 1992.

She had left her home in Balham at about 9:15 a.m., driven to Wimbledon Common for one of her regular walks with Alex and parked her car by the Windmill. She took the Windmill Ride bridle path, young Alex at her side, Molly romping on the grass, to enjoy the summer sunshine while strolling through the park. It was the 'playful slow walk', said Mr Boyce, of a mother and son at peace with the world. Several witnesses would be called who had seen them that morning. One woman and her husband remarked how stunning she looked, with her hair pinned up, holding the hand of a little boy they said was 'dark-haired and cute'. And Mr Adrian Lister, a regular visitor to the common, was particularly entranced. 'She looked so happy, tossing her hair and laughing,' he said. 'I smiled at her and she smiled back.' He leaned on his car and turned to watch mother and son disappearing across the grass.

The evident joy of mother and child was disastrously short-lived, ending some 35 minutes later in the densely wooded copse where she was seized by an unknown attacker and brutally slaughtered as the little boy watched. Mr Boyce was precise about times — they were, of course, of the greatest importance in this case in the light of Stagg's protestations about when he had, or had not, been on the common that morning. Rachel, said Mr Boyce, was last seen alive at 10:20 a.m., clearly remembered by a reliable witness, the actor Mr McKern. Her body was found exactly fifteen minutes later — 10:35 a.m. Alex, bare-chested, was hugging her body. Rachel had been stabbed all over her chest, abdomen and back, her throat cut so viciously that her head was almost severed. Her hands revealed protective wounds where she had tried to fight off the killer. Her jeans and panties were round her ankles and her bra had been partially pulled down to expose her nipples, clearly indicating a sexual motive. It was likely that she had been confonted on the pathway, threatened with a knife, forcibly marched or dragged to the base of a nearby tree, knifed repeatedly then turned on her side and sexually assaulted.

The details were familiar to many of those in court — the detectives in the case, the legal representatives on both sides, reporters who had written about the appalling crime. Related in Mr Boyce's calm, unemotional voice in the confines of a courtroom, they sounded no less chilling. Stagg, said Mr Boyce, had been arrested on suspicion of murdering Rachel once before but had denied any involvement, saying he had left the common before the murder and gone home to sleep. The Crown, he said, was now in a position to shatter his alibi. And, he said, he would call evidence from Paul Britton and Lizzie James which suggested that Stagg had a sexually deviant personality disorder which matched exactly those characteristics shown by the killer of Rachel Nickell.

First to dispute Stagg's claim that he was back home by 8:30 a.m. and safely asleep on his sofa on the morning of the murder was Alton Estate neighbour Mrs Susan Gale. She clearly remembered seeing him, with Brandy, at around nine o'clock that day. She'd left home herself at about 8:50 for a shorter than usual walk on the common with her two dogs, a seven-year-old labrador and a puppy, and had spotted Stagg near the A3 underpass, on Jerry's Hill, as she returned home to take her elderly mother to draw her pension. 'I think he waved at me,' she said. They always grabbed their dogs, she said, in case a fight started. She had known Stagg for nine years and recognised his distinctive walk. He was wearing some sort of bag around his waist — a black 'bum bag' she thought. She arrived back home at 9:35 a.m. and, despite the shock of hearing of Rachel's murder later that day, thought nothing more about her casual meeting with Colin Stagg. Until, that was, she saw the *Crimewatch* videofit two months later, showing a suspect the police were anxious to find. 'It reminded me at once of Colin Stagg,' she said. 'It was a very close likeness'. She called the police.

Pauline Fleming said she saw a man, aged about 29 or 30, walking briskly on the common near the scene of the murder at 9:30 a.m. 'I thought he was someone going off to work,' she said. 'He was walking with a purpose . . . as if he was late for something. He was carrying a dark bag in his right hand.'

Jane Harriman, blonde, pretty, well spoken and smartly dressed, was a powerful witness for the prosecution. If the killer was Colin Stagg her canny observations had produced a quite remarkable likeness of him for the police. He looked a lot different now, by accident or design, but she wasn't asked to point him out. Dock identifications are now a thing of the past in British courts. She barely glanced at Stagg from the witness stand as she told how she went to Brixton police station — where Scotland Yard has a specialist identification suite — to take part in an ID parade after the *Crimewatch* programme, and her picture, most of all, had resulted in Colin Stagg's first arrest. 'I picked out one of the ten men in the line-up as being the man I had seen on the common,' she said. It was Colin Stagg. Next day she saw a TV news bulletin showing Stagg running from Wimbledon Magistrates' Court after being fined for indecent exposure. He was definitely the man on the common, she said. Then she saw a report and photo in the *Daily Mail* which left her in no doubt whatsoever that her memory of 15 July was accurate. There was, she said, absolutely no doubt in her mind. The man she had seen on Wimbledon Common, the man who had made her feel worried and a little frightened, was unquestionably Colin Stagg, she told the magistrate.

'Have you ever made a mistake in identifying anyone?' asked Mr Sturman.

'Not that I can think,' replied Mrs Harriman.

'Never, for instance, seen someone you thought was

a friend and it wasn't?' inquired the defence lawyer.

'Possibly, yes,' she agreed.

'Did you have difficulty picking out the man at the identification parade?'

'I didn't have any difficulty after I had calmed down.' The trauma of the identification parade had clearly upset her at the time, strong as her character appeared to be, but no-one was surprised by that.

'Were you ever told Mr Stagg was a strong suspect for the murder?' asked Mr Sturman.

'No, not that I can remember,' said Mrs Harriman.

Was she, asked Mr Sturman, someone who likes to be exact? 'I like to be accurate,' replied Mrs Harriman, and those in court could see that she was a woman who knew her own mind. She wasn't particularly studying the man on the common, she said, but always liked to keep an eye open for possible danger, especially when she was with the children, and he had made her edgy. There was no doubt, she asserted, that she had seen him at one stage with a belt, or something similar, tied loosely round his waist, an inch or two above his trouser band.

'I would like you,' said the defence barrister, 'to look at Mr Stagg in the dock and describe his nose.'

There was a moment or two's hesitation as she looked carefully at Stagg then said, 'Long and thin, straight.'

'Thank you,' said Mr Sturman, without further comment or clarification. Bags, belts and noses were clearly going to be important issues in the case of the Crown versus Colin Francis Stagg.

The third day of the hearing saw Mr Sturman

looking bullish as he sipped a morning cup of tea in the court cafeteria. 'I think they've got the wrong man,' he said confidently. 'It is going to be a very interesting trial.' Even at this early stage in the committal proceedings, he obviously felt the case would be sent to the Old Bailey for trial by jury, despite his submissions, but was clearly set to give the prosecution a run for their money, here and now. He discussed briefly with pressmen the case of east Londoner George Ince, cleared in the seventies of a particularly brutal murder at the Barn nightspot in Braintree, Essex, after police were found to have shown photographs of the wanted suspect to witnesses before his arrest. When Ince finally surrendered to police and was put in identification parades, the witnesses found themselves identifying the man they had seen in the photos, not the man who was at the Barn on the night of the murder when owner's wife Muriel Patience was shot at point-blank range and her daughter Beverley badly injured. Ince, the lover of former gangster Charlie Kray's wife, Dolly, was acquitted (many thought luckily) and the police were reluctant to reopen the case, believing he had cheated justice. Then, more than six months later, the two real killers were arrested, still in possession of the murder weapon. It became obvious that George Ince had come within a whisker of a monumental miscarriage of justice through the police identification system and that changes were needed. The case quickly led to new police regulations banning witnesses from seeing photographs of suspects prior to identification parades. It was a legal milestone at the time. Mr Sturman was a friend and business associate of the solicitor who had so brilliantly conducted the Ince defence, Ralph Haeems. Identification issues were certain to be high on the agenda in the case of Colin Stagg too.

Mr Boyce began piecing together the life and times of Colin Stagg with evidence from witnesses who knew him before, on and after the day of Rachel's murder. Butcher Patrick Heanan, whose shop is in Petersfield Rise, Alton Estate, served Stagg a couple of times a week. 'He is a creature of habit,' he said. 'He's never without his dog. Dogs love him. He seems to attract them. He's very much a loner and never talks to anyone in the street. On the day of the murder he came in about 11:15 a.m. The helicopter was overhead and I thought at first they were looking for a lost child. Colin came in and said a body had been found on the common. His behaviour seemed normal, although he had never just come in for a chat before.' What the court did not hear was a telling phrase Mr Heanan was said to have uttered to detectives when they first interviewed him . . . that he was so alarmed about Stagg's demeanour that he had thought to himself, 'Oh my God, Colin, what have you done?' Police were disappointed that the butcher was not prepared to repeat this in his written statement, to be used in the prosecution evidence submitted to the court.

Newsagent Yadnesh Patel, whose shop is also in Petersfield Rise, employed Stagg on an early-morning newspaper round. 'He's a real loner,' he said. 'He never opens conversations and just replies with a single word. He told me he had been at university.' Stagg bought a bar of chocolate from Mr Patel at about 12:45 p.m. on the day of the murder. He said the police were stopping people from going on the common and he couldn't walk his dog. 'He seemed quite excited . . . more excited than I had ever seen him,' said the newsagent.

Lillian Avid, the nervous neighbour who had asked Colin Stagg if he was the killer, was asked by Mr Sturman if it was purely her instinct at work. 'By his actions, I was thinking, "Did he do it? Did he do it?"' she replied.

'Did you think he was so clean because he had just washed the blood off?' asked Mr Sturman.

'I had a feeling he had just changed his clothes, he was so clean. I felt he must have changed his clothes if he had done it,' replied Mrs Avid.

Had she heard a profile of the Rachel killer read out on *Crimewatch* by either a detective or by presenter Nick Ross? Characteristics like the killer being a loner? Yes, said Mrs Avid, she had. Did the photofit which was shown match anyone else on the Alton Estate? 'No one that I know,' said the plump and homely Mrs Avid. What about Stagg's nose, enquired Mr Sturman. 'I've never looked,' she said, clearly bemused by the line of questioning. And his eyes? 'Sort of smiley, sparkly eyes,' she recalled, glancing at Stagg in the dock. 'But I don't know the colour.'

Christine Perrior employed Stagg as a part-time gardener at her home on the Alton Estate. Like everyone else she was told diplomatically by Mr Boyce that she would be battling against the rumble of trains outside as she gave her evidence. The noise was, at times, so bad that it could drown a vital sentence here and there. However, the lawyers made sure nothing was lost. If anything was indistinct first time, it was repeated to ensure total accuracy in every detail of the evidence.

'I didn't speak to Colin very much,' said Mrs Perrior. 'I used to let him in the back gate, plug in the extension lead for the lawn mower and let him get on with the work.' For 45 minutes' work Stagg got £10 — a useful earner on top of his dole and social security allowances. He turned up for work the day after the murder, by prior arrangement, and started the mowing after sipping a cold drink given to him by Christine Perrior. 'As I handed it to him I said, "It's terrible, that murder on the common." He said he usually walked his dog there every morning but for some reason he hadn't that day. I said to him: "Whoever could do a thing like that, especially in front of a child? He must be sick." I said they needed stringing up or shooting. He said he hadn't seen anything . . . but didn't really finish the conversation. It just fizzled out.' Stagg, the man who supposedly loved all creatures great and small, then popped home for some ant powder to kill a swarm of the insects invading Christine's garden.

Mr Sturman was curious as to how her statement had been made fourteen months after the conversation with Stagg took place, implying, perhaps, that she had jumped on the bandwagon after his second arrest. It was quite simple, she said, police had carried out door-to-door inquiries on the estate and she had been happy to tell them about her relationship with Stagg. She certainly had nothing to hide. And was he excitable or upset that day? No, there was nothing unusual about him, she said. To no-one's surprise, by now, Mr Sturman then turned once again to Stagg's nose. How would you describe it, he asked. She looked puzzled for a few seconds then replied, 'Slightly thick.' It was a line of questioning that was already becoming repetitive but it was being pursued with such relish by Jim Sturman that no-one doubted its eventual significance.

Neighbour Cheryl Lewis — from 12 Ibsley Gardens — was another who took a charitable view of Stagg's predicament after he had been arrested and released first time.

'I believed that because he had been freed, he must be innocent. The way I looked at it, he didn't need me slamming the door in his face. I made him welcome in my home. He was getting a lot of people calling him names and shouting abuse at him. I used to see him more or less every day and he came most weekends for a cup of tea, always with his dog Brandy. He would sometimes stay until 12 o'clock or 1 a.m., no particular time. Sometimes I would be on my own with him, sometimes there would be other people there, friends of mine. He told me a few things about his time in police custody. He said that every time he tried to go to sleep someone would wake him up and ask him if he wanted anything. He told me he had been shown photos of Rachel and described them to me. He said it looked as if her head had been removed from her body — that she had been decapitated — and then placed on her shoulders and that she was lying in a foetal position. He insisted he didn't do the murder. He said the police had told him he had been seen stabbing a tree on the common, which he denied. He said the police had told him he had seen Rachel on the common, which he also refuted. But he told me that he had seen her over there. He said he had seen Rachel sunbathing by a pond, but I'm not sure which one. Apparently she used to go to the common quite a lot. I got the impression he had seen her more than once. She used to have a dog with her. I asked him why he kept going back. He said, "If someone accused me of doing something like that . . ." then seemed to become upset and stopped.'

In his cross-examination, Mr Sturman hit Cheryl with the nose quiz straight away. How would she describe it? She looked a trifle embarrassed as she answered, 'I don't really know.' And his eyes? They were fixed, she agreed. 'He looks straight into you.' She said she had made a statement to the police about Stagg after discussing the *Crimewatch* programme with a neighbour. She had never said one hundred per cent that the photofit was Colin, but it did resemble him, she said. She had told Stagg he was mad to keep going back to the common but he had said why should other people dictate what he should do. He was innocent, he maintained.

Another of the Ibsley Gardens residents, Tina Woodsell, regularly saw Stagg taking his dog for a walk, sometimes with a lead hanging over his shoulders. And she had seen him with an old and battered black bag his dad had left when he died. It wasn't, M Sturman suggested, a shiny PVC bag as described by some witnesses allegedly being carried by the suspected killer. No, it wasn't, she said. It was old, battered and with a pattern on the front. The full-length *Crimewatch* videofit, she said, did not give sufficient details to suggest it was Colin Stagg — it was the characteristics of the likely killer, as defined by the psychologist, which prompted her to contact the police. The second picture, just of the suspect's face, was like him, she said. And, on the subject of faces, would she please describe Stagg's nose. Another puzzled pause and she said, 'Well, basically straight. Nothing unusual about it.'

'And the photofit,' said Mr Sturman. 'Does it look at all like a Mr Martin Butler?'

'No, it doesn't.'

'And do you know Martin Butler?'

'Yes.'

He was, in fact, another neighbour of Stagg's, and was said to bear more than a passing resemblance to him. He had already been elimininated from police inquiries.

Mrs Karma Leonard had seen Stagg with a PVC-look bag on about three different occasions prior to the murder. But afterwards, she said, she never saw him with it once. And, she said, she had seen him out walking without Brandy the dog — something he claimed he never did. A small, but significant point, the prosecution submitted, in the context of events on the common on 15 July 1992.

The one-time family friend Tina Burridge — who had changed her name to Molloy by deed poll by the time she was called to give evidence — probably knew Stagg as well as anyone was ever likely to from their cosy chats over a cup of coffee. She was asked by Mr Sturman: 'Knowing him as you do, and forgetting that he is here in this courtroom, do you think he is capable of murder?'

'No, I don't,' she replied, then added, 'but are we sure of anybody?'

'Indeed,' said Mr Sturman weightily. 'Did you,' he asked Tina, a doleful-looking woman in a black leather jacket who had been too ill to attend as a witness earlier in the proceedings, 'get the impression that Stagg was "absolutely desperate" to lose his virginity?'

'Yes,' she said, he had made no secret of the fact.

Mr Sturman was out to prove that Stagg, embarrassed and frustrated by his virginity, was so anxious to have sex with a woman that he had invented the obscene fantasies sent to Lizzie James simply in the hope that it would persuade her to go to bed with him. It wasn't exactly Mills and Boon but did it make him a killer? It was the start of a defence attack on the police operation that was to have astonishing repercussions for every person involved in the Rachel Nickell inquiry.

An Act of Sadism

Dr Richard Shepherd knows more than most about death and depravity. As a leading Home Office pathologist, he has investigated more than 750 suspicious deaths over the past ten years — murders, suicides, accidents, or the unfathomable. The call to Wimbledon Common on the morning of 15 July 1992 was routine, if such a phrase could ever really apply to a career that deals exclusively in death. The first call, oddly, had been for police to attend the scene of an attack on an 'old woman with a young boy'. Nothing could have been further from the truth. This was a young woman in the prime of life.

Professionally Dr Shepherd showed little emotion as he arrived at 12:18 that afternoon to be told by Detective Chief Inspector Wickerson at the murder scene: 'It's a nasty one, doctor.' Personally, he must have felt as sickened as the police officers as he began his examination of Rachel's knife-ravaged body. Nothing had been moved. She lay as the killer had left her. The police were just finishing a video film of the body and the surrounding area for future reference in the investigation. Dr Shepherd, consultant pathologist at Guys and St Thomas's Hospitals in London, began by taking the temperature of Rachel's body to assist in determining the precise time of death. This was, in fact, to give a totally misleading estimate because the body had cooled far more quickly than usual due to the excessive loss of blood. The doctor said the murder could have happened up to ten hours earlier — any time between 4 a.m. and 11 a.m. This threw the police off-balance temporarily as they were certain it had happened much more recently, around midmorning. The estimate was later rectified by Dr Shepherd after he had recalculated the time of death more accurately after taking into consideration the exceptionally high blood loss due to the massive wounds that had been inflicted on Rachel's body.

Called as the first of the Crown's key expert witnesses on the fourth day of the committal hearing, Dr Shepherd said he took swabs from the vaginal and anal areas for forensic examination. The police had hoped these would reveal body samples — semen, blood, hair or saliva — from which a DNA 'genetic fingerprint' of the killer could be produced. This was the miracle weapon police had used to solve hundreds of murders and rapes since it was pioneered by Professor Alec Jeffreys of Leicester University nine years earlier — one of the most important developments in crimefighting techniques this century. The discovery that no two people, except for identical twins, have the same DNA cell pattern revolutionised the forensic detection of killers and sex attackers worldwide and has been used to resolve thousands of disputed paternity cases. A single hair root can give a complete genetic profile, showing up under laboratory microscopes like a supermarket bar code — every one distinctive, every one different. The odds against a DNA 'fingerprint' being wrong are more than 30 million to one. Unfortunately, in the case of Rachel Nickell the killer had left no traces from which a DNA reading could be made, despite the fact that it was clearly a sex attack of the most frenzied nature. If Rachel had been raped, as it was initially believed, the attacker had not ejaculated to leave behind telltale samples of semen. Nor were there any traces of skin or hair caught under her fingernails when she may have tried to fight him off.

Dr Shepherd, a tall, precise, angular man, noted that the anus was widely dilated but there was no evidence of bleeding from either the anal or vaginal areas. There was, Dr Shepherd told the court, a mass of stab wounds visible on the body, which was lying between separate pools of blood. There was little more he could do at the scene and he deferred further examination until Rachel's corpse had been taken to St George's Hospital mortuary.

There, in the presence of Superintendent Bassett, Chief Inspector Wickerson and the coroner, Dr Dole, he began the post mortem that was to tell the police just what sort of monster they were dealing with.

There were, said the pathologist, a total of 49 stab wounds — nineteen back injuries, 26 to the chest and abdomen, three to the neck which had virtually severed her head, and one defensive wound to her left hand where she had fought briefly but vainly to fend off the killer. There were two bruises on her forehead and one on her chin. Many of the stab wounds had pierced her heart, lungs and liver. The murder weapon was probably a single-edged sheath knife with a brass hilt, he said.

An album of photos of Rachel's injuries was compiled by Dr Shepherd for eventual use in criminal proceedings. It was a distressing but vital requirement that a jury would one day probably have to see such tragic pictures, along with the police videos of the body and murder scene, already shown to the magistrate on a TV screen specially set up in court.

Dr Shepherd was to be a detective as much as a medic in helping the police to determine the probable course of events as Rachel met her brutal death. He noted that there were several areas of heavy bloodstaining at the murder scene, indicating that Rachel's body had been moved by the killer into the place where she was found, under the silver birch tree, her naked buttocks exposed. He prepared a sketch plan showing the main area of bloodstaining under the body, another area a few yards away, and separate rings in between. The amount of bloodstaining at the murder scene, he explained, would be affected by a number of factors — the nature of the injuries which were bleeding, the heart rate, the blood pressure, and the time the victim was in one particular area. Rachel's jeans, he said, were coated in blood almost exclusively in the upper front area. There was significant spotting of blood on the back of the lower leg area and there were fresh mud stains on the lower front of the jeans. The pattern of bloodstaining, on the clothes and at the murder site, showed that the attack had happened in four phases, after the killer had forced Rachel from the footpath into the wood, goading her with painful prods of his knife.

Phase 1:   The killer struck the first fatal blows to the neck at the spot where the largest area of bloodstaining was found, some yards away from the body. The relative absence of bloodstaining on the lower portions of Rachel's jeans indicated that she had been forced to her knees at this stage. It was a harrowing scenario. Perhaps her family might have had some small consolation if they could have been told that she had at least died swiftly and painlessly. Unfortunately it was not so. Dr Shepherd said that the savage injuries to the neck were of a type and depth that would have resulted in 'severe pain and shock'. Damage to the muscles of the neck and to the cartilages of the larynx were likely to have prevented her from crying out or screaming for help. From the kneeling position, she would have tumbled forward on to her face, with the haemorrhage from the ghastly neck wounds causing the first pool of blood on the ground. The most likely position of the assailant was behind Rachel, with the knife in his right hand. Rachel's jeans and knickers were still in their proper place at this point.

Phase 2: Rachel was moved, or she staggered, towards the base of the silver birch. The presence of leaf mould on the back of her body and the back of her T-shirt was consistent with her lying on her back at this stage, facing the base of the tree, with the killer lunging at her body with his knife.

Phase 3: The killer tried to remove Rachel's jeans and pants. The leaf mould on her buttocks indicated that she was still on her back at this point. 'Either during, or after, the partial removal of the clothing, Rachel's body was turned and pulled away to the approximate position where she was discovered,' he said. The killer had clearly continued to rain frantic blows on her body.

Phase 4: The killer sexually violated Rachel's body after pulling her jeans and pants down to her lower calves. 'Anal penetration would have taken place when she was either dead or at a point so close to death, that she would not have responded to penetration,' said Dr Shepherd. Other blows were probably inflicted with the killer's knife after the sexual assault. The pathologist told the court: 'In my opinion the minimum length of time needed to inflict all the injuries on Rachel's body would be in the region of three minutes.'

A wonderful life had been wiped out in three minutes of unimaginable brutality on a sunny summer morning in a public park. Dr Shepherd's necessarily dispassionate tones could not alleviate the sheer horror of it all, compounded as it was by the knowledge that Rachel's little boy must have watched every blow, every perverted act, before the killer fled off into the bushes.

Dr Shepherd said at least thirteen wounds had definitely been inflicted after death on the right side of the chest and abdomen with another nine to the left side of the chest possibly caused after death. There were five deep penetrative wounds to the lungs and three to the heart, any one of which would have killed Rachel. The lack of significant defence wounds suggested that Rachel had been given no chance to defend herself from the killer's onslaught. Abrasions to the right side of her chin were difficult to determine, said the pathologist. They might have been caused by the rough application of a hand or material, or by her collapsing on to the ground.

Dr Shepherd's detective work helped to explain how the killer could have fled from the scene with virtually no bloodstains on his clothing at all — a fact which had looked impossible when the extent of Rachel's injuries was initially revealed. Only the neck injuries had bled externally, sending blood pumping on to her clothes and on to the ground. As Rachel's heart stopped beating and her life ebbed away, other wounds had bled internally. Dr Shepherd said that with the assailant standing behind Rachel and with no significant close contact between them, it was 'extremely possible' that the only easily visible bloodstaining on the assailant would be on his hands. This made the sighting of the man washing his hands in a stream just after the murder doubly significant. Any other pinprick bloodstains on the killer could be detected only by forensic examination and would not have been visible to the naked eye. Sightings of the mystery man with a bag had already raised the possibility that the killer had embarked on a premeditated murder mission, taking a change of clothing with him.

Had the killer carried out the anal assault with bloodied hands, said Dr Shepherd, there would have been blood deposits left in that area. The dilation of the anus, he said, had been caused by the fact that the muscles had ceased to work after death to perform a normal retraction after penetration. It was an act of shameful depravity.

Colin Stagg barely glanced at the pathologist across the room as he sat, looking down, in the witness box. His mum and stepdad shifted uncomfortably on the wooden seats in the public gallery. They must surely have wondered from time to time whether Colin could have done this and then, no doubt, dismissed it from their minds. Not the Colin they knew, they had assured anybody who asked, he couldn't possibly have done it. It had to be someone else, they repeated over and over.

Mr Sturman was anxious to know whether there had been any collusion between Dr Shepherd and Mr Britton in coming to their respective conclusions; whether they might somehow have got together to manufacture evidence against Stagg. 'I have never met Mr Britton at any time,' said Dr Shepherd, 'and I have not discussed any aspect of this case with him. I have seen no reports prepared by him.' He had, he said, seen only a handwritten report by Robert Ressler, which touched on the subject of offender profiling. 'I am aware Mr Britton is involved in this case,' said the pathologist, 'but it has been made clear to me that I must form my own conclusions. The reports of Mr Britton and his conclusions were, and still are, unknown to me.'

Had he heard, asked Mr Sturman, about a mortuary assistant's boyfriend 'blabbing' about the injuries to Rachel Nickell — giving out details which Stagg said he had heard on the gossip grapevine around the Alton Estate soon after the murder. The pathologist replied, 'I was unaware that the boyfriend, or anyone else connected with the inquiry, had to be warned concerning my professional examination or the injuries that were present on Rachel Nickell.'

He said the object which had been inserted into Rachel's anus could have been an animate or inanimate object. 'Within this group I would include a penis,' he said.

Dr Shepherd confirmed his belief that if the assailant had been standing in front of Rachel when he slashed her throat, he would have been soaked in blood. 'But the angle of the throat wounds is such that I think it is more likely that the assailant was standing behind Rachel at the time,' he said.

It would be hard to imagine a more terrifying murder, or the motivations behind such a demented act. To Paul Britton such depravity is everyday work. As a consultant clinical psychologist for over ten years, he has seen every extremity of human behaviour possible and delved into the deepest abyss of the mind. Since 1986 he had been the head of the Trent Regional Forensic Psychology Service and also taught post-graduate students at the Universities of Leicester and Hull. For a decade, he had assisted the police in building up offender profiles and had helped to plan strategies for catching sexually deviant criminals. Recently, he had been asked to join FBI specialists in designing and teaching at centres in the USA and Britain. He was the organiser of the 1992 Trevi conference on offender profiling. A confident, quietly-spoken man with an unswerving belief in his own professionalism, he was among the leading flagbearers for offender profiling in the world. Psychology, he told the court, was a well-established discipline, based on medical principles, which had been practised in the UK since the end of World War Two and granted a royal charter in 1965. It was on this psychological knowledge, he said, that the art of offender profiling was built.

From his experience, said Mr Britton, there would be no doubt that the killer of Rachel Nickell was one of a tiny number of perverts in Britain whose sexual satisfaction was gained by acts of sadism, domination and fear, culminating in sexual frenzy and death. The covert operation involving Lizzie James, he said, was devised by him with the specific provision that Stagg would automatically eliminate himself if he failed to react in a manner expected of the Rachel Nickel killer. At the end of the six-month operation, he said, Stagg's sexuality was indistinguishable from the offender profile of the murderer, which he had drafted from information available a few weeks after the killing and prior to Stagg becoming a suspect. The fantasies contained in Stagg's letters to Lizzie and his taped conversations with her, Britton said, indicated a man obsessed with gratuitous violence and deviant sex. His opinion of Stagg's fantasies was: 'The imagery, contained and predicted, is intense, very clearly described, quite specific, and the intensity and clarity are both consistent with fantasies that are enacted rather than masturbated to.' This was based, he said, on his knowledge of serious sexual offenders and the relevant literature in clinical and forensic psychology available to him.

Mr Sturman took a somewhat more cynical view of psychology and offender profiling. It was not, he ventured, an exact science and was based in part on pure guesswork. Mr Britton, needless to say, disagreed. Both men were aware that, should it be sent for trial at the Old Bailey, this case was the first in which offender profiling would form the main plank of the prosecution evidence and it was certain to be contentious.

'Is Colin Stagg mentally ill?' asked Mr Sturman.

'I don't know, I've never examined him,' said Mr Britton.

Exactly the point, Mr Sturman indicated. 'If you've never examined him, how can you draw any positive conclusions?' he asked. 'Does he suffer from an abnormality within the terms of the Homicide Act of 1957?'

'I can't tell you that.'

Because he had been unable to examine any individual in connection with his analysis of the deviant sexual fantasy life characterising the murder of Rachel Nickell, said Mr Britton, he had used the term 'personality disturbance' as a general term rather than a specific psychological conclusion. 'To safely recognise a particular personality disorder it is important to know, among other things, the length of time the individual has experienced, or been subject to, the phenomena.'

One of the more curious facts to emerge about the particular deviancy suffered by Rachel's killer was that it tends first to affect young men in their early teens, arouses intense and violent fantasies for many years, then finally manifests itself in a murderous attack at the age of 28 or thereabouts. Those affected — thankfully just a tiny sub-group of the deviant population — are walking timebombs. These, said Mr Britton, were concrete facts which had emerged from studies of many case histories of such abnormalities.

Quietly spoken, and often competing with the noise of mainline and suburban trains thundering past on the railway line outside, Mr Britton told the court he was aware of the code of conduct governing the questioning by police of a vulnerable person, when a responsible adult must be present. 'I don't know if Mr Stagg is such a person,' he said. 'What I can tell you is that the operation I designed was specifically constructed so as to present whoever was to be the subject of the operation with a series of ladders they would have to climb in a conceptual sense, rather than a slippery slope that any person, especially a vulnerable person, would inexorably slide down should they be pushed.' Was he satisfied that Stagg was telling the truth in his letters to Lizzie, not simply saying anything in the hope of bedding her and losing his virginity? 'I saw nothing,' said Mr Britton, 'in either the correspondence or transcripts, or indeed anything else concerned with Mr Stagg, which indicated otherwise than the fantasies were genuinely held and, in addition, I would say the fantasies he described are entirely consistent with genuine fantasies reported by people who have sexual deviations. The fantasies are entirely consistent with being quite genuine and entirely inconsistent with being a mere pretence in order to entice someone into bed with him.'

'But a lot of quite normal people have sexual fantasies, don't they?' argued Mr Sturman.

'They do,' agreed the psychologist. 'Large sections of the population fantasise, but don't put it into effect. I would estimate a significant proportion fantasise about making love in the open air — not less than 25 per cent.'

And how many get their sexual thrills through rear-entry vaginal intercourse? 'That,' said Mr Britton, 'would be an element in the repertoire of a reasonable proportion of married or cohabiting couples.' For instance, he said, part of his everyday work was a special clinic held, with colleagues, for non-deviant couples who experienced some form of sexual difficulty. The work of the clinic required that each partner separately gave a full sexual history which involved their sexual practices and performances. Rear-entry vaginal penetration or intercourse was reported by about 5 per cent of those people. The proportion might be higher in the general population. 'And may I say to you it would be precisely for this sort of reason that a close and detailed specification of the offender's sexual deviant fantasies had to be considered rather than aspects which were much more generally evident in the general population,' he said.

Had Mr Britton made written predictions from time to time about how Stagg might react if he was the killer? 'I don't think so,' he said. 'I might have, but it was mostly graphs which would depict the expected path of both the deviant sexual behaviour and sexual violence, together with their intensities against the murderer's level of self-preservation and caution.' Did he make notes of any such predictions in such an important case, which he might like to produce in court? 'No,' said Mr Britton. 'I made any observations direct to police officers present at the time. It is my usual practice, when advising police forces, to consult in this way unless I am specifically asked to do otherwise.'

Would Mr Britton agree that there was a lot of academic concern about the discipline of offender profiling? There were, he said, one or two dissenting voices. Offender profiling, as it was developing in the UK today, he said, was based on three main strands — detective expertise, the development of databases, and professional psychological expertise. It relies on all three elements to different extents in different cases. It was certainly the case that databases — the storing of case histories on computer — was still at an early stage. But it promised to be, eventually, the most important stride forward. Preliminary stages were being undertaken in Surrey — at the university and at police headquarters — in London with the Metropolitan Police sexual assault unit and in Derbyshire where police now hold the largest such system in the country, which deals solely with abducted, missing or murdered children. 'As a consequence of work in these areas,' said Mr Britton, 'work is being undertaken on behalf of the Home Office and the Association of Chief Police Officers towards the development of more powerful analytical tools.'

'How many murders of young women in broad daylight with a young child did you analyse?' asked Mr Sturman.

'There isn't another which matches that precisely,' said Mr Britton.

'Would you call this an overkill murder?' inquired

Mr Sturman.

'I don't use the word "overkill",' said the psychologist, explaining that it was a term used by the FBI in America where a victim suffers twenty or more stab wounds. They would then say that the offender was likely to be known to the victim, but where there were only nineteen or fewer wounds they wouldn't be. 'We are not altogether persuaded of that in the UK,' said Mr Britton.

An overkill murder — like the term or not was strongly suggestive of a personal relationship between killer and victim? inquired the lawyer.

'No,' said Mr Britton, 'I wouldn't agree. I am saying exactly the opposite.' The FBI now recognised that they might have got it wrong in that area and were in the course of rectifying it by using professional psychologists in their analysis, rather than just FBI operatives.

Mr Britton said he had analysed hundreds of sexual fantasies and been involved in 60 to 70 investigations with police in which a significant proportion required sexual analysis. Of these, ten to twenty were sexually-motivated murders. 'As far as I know, I haven't ever got a profile completely wrong,' he said. He denied that the use of the occult and the cover of Lizzie as a cat sitter had been deliberately introduced into the covert operation to 'strike a chord' with Stagg. 'In my original profile there was no specific mention of the occult but I said the murderer would have unusual and solitary hobbies. In designing the cover story of the confidante, I wanted to be sure that it was plausible and based upon cases from which I could provide a detailed background.' A roving cat sitter with sado-masochistic tendencies who had been involved in a ritual murder in her teens was not everyone's idea of an everyday pen pal's background. But then he wasn't dealing with everyday people here.

Mr Britton said Stagg's letters had clearly indicated excitement at the prospect of violent death. 'From Mr Stagg's correspondence,' he said, 'I would expect elements of sexual frenzy which could result in the death of the other participant. It is also the case that Mr Stagg reported sexual excitement at the contemplation of just such an attack on Rachel Nickell. The Lizzie James cover story was designed to produce a response to such stimulus from a sexually deviant personality. It was devised that way precisely because it was such an unusual sexual deviant persona.' The chances of two men with the same sexual deviancy being together in the same place at the same time is utterly remote, he said, unless that place was a special hospital or a prison. He said he had not been asked to prepare profiles or give detailed consideration to any of the other 30 or so men questioned in connection with the murder and subsequently released.

How many people were likely to have responded to Lizzie James in the same way as Colin Stagg? asked Mr Sturman. 'I would say the proportion that would produce the fantasies, the detail, the intensity, the aggression and who could give precise knowledge of the disposition of the body of Rachel Nickell, would be vanishingly small,' said the psychologist.

'Vanishingly small,' repeated the lawyer, as if he wasn't quite sure what it meant.

In his profiling, said Mr Sturman, Mr Britton had listed eight characteristics he would expect to find in the killer of Rachel Nickell — including an attraction to young adult women. What proportion of normal healthy young men are likely to fantasise about normal healthy young women? asked Mr Sturman. 'Most of them, I would expect,' conceded the psychologist.

Another characteristic listed by Mr Britton was men masturbating over the thought of using a woman as a 'sexual object'. How unusual was that? Not unusual at all, agreed Mr Britton — about 40 to 50 per cent of males would do it. And was it common for people who fantasise to build up an imaginary relationship with the person they were thinking about? Yes, it was. The number of men displaying sadistic tendencies? — 'small'. Using a knife in fantasies? — 'extremely rare'. Physical control? — 'not common'. Verbal abuse? — 'not common'.

As an expert in fantasies, asked Mr Sturman, had Mr Britton read *My Secret Garden* by Nancy Friday? No, he hadn't. Mr Sturman looked surprised. 'Were you even aware of its existence?' he asked.

'Yes, I was.'

As an expert in the field of fantasy, did he not feel it was his professional duty to read this?

'No'.

What about fantasies involving anal assault? asked Mr Sturman, how unusual were they? — 'extremely uncommon'. Female fear? — 'not often'. And was there anything in Stagg's letters which indicated killing? — 'The signs of sexual frenzy were evident and such activity could end in the death of the female participant.' But doesn't Stagg approach the relationship with Lizzie with an almost teenage naivety, hoping for the chance of a long-lasting relationship? 'I don't think that is restricted to teenagers,' said Mr Britton. But they don't normally fall in love, replied Mr Sturman. 'But I think a lot of people fall in lust that way,' said the psychologist, heavily emphasising the word 'lust'.

What if Paul Britton was entirely wrong about Stagg and he was just someone who was excited by pornography? 'His behaviour is consistent with fantasies I see in serious sexual offenders,' maintained Mr Britton. 'If he had not responded to this operation it would have had no value. As a clinical psychologist it would have been my duty to say that he had not exhibited or demonstrated the behaviour I would have expected from the killer of Rachel Nickell.' Suppose for one minute, Mr Sturman requested, that Rachel Nickell knew her killer. Would the whole basis of his analysis collapse? 'From my knowledge of the scene, and the evidence so far, I believe the sexual life of her killer remains the same, irrespective of the degree of knowledge of the person who killed her.'

After two days of evidence and questioning, Paul Britton left the witness box unshakable in his belief that Colin Stagg's behaviour matched exactly that of the killer of Rachel Nickell. If he wasn't right on this one, a lifetime's dedication in this complex field of psychology might look like a pointless waste of time.

Heads You Lose

Lizzie James, the reluctant star of the police undercover operation which had resulted in Colin Stagg's arrest, sat just twenty feet away from the man who had fallen so madly in love with her. Stagg squirmed uncomfortably for a minute or two on his dock seat, then picked up a pen and scribbled a quick note to his lawyer, handing it across with something of a flourish as if he wanted to be sure everyone in court saw it. Jim Sturman read the note, nodded towards Stagg, then placed it with the ever-growing pile of paperwork on the bench beside him — a mound of defence documentation which they hoped would eventually prove that Stagg was an innocent man.

Lizzie had slipped into court during the lunch break, through the magistrates' entrance, and was safely hidden from public gaze as she sat on a chair in the witness box ready to start her evidence. A wooden screen protected her from all but the view of the magistrate, the lawyers and Colin Stagg himself. In a security operation unprecedented at Wimbledon, paper covered all the courtroom windows from unwanted intrusion. Lizzie was told to remain seated at all times in case her head became visible when she stood up. The doors were locked and police were positioned inside and out as she began what was expected to be some of the most compelling evidence ever heard in a British court of law. Just a voice emerged from behind the screen — well educated, the slightest touch, perhaps, of a north-country background, as prosecutor Boyce began to take her through the evidence that was so crucial to the Crown case.

She was, she said, an undercover specialist who had been given the pseudonym Lizzie James specifically for the Stagg operation because she wanted her true identity to remain secret. She would, she said, expect to be used in further covert operations in the future and, for that reason, wished for the anonymity of the protective screens in court. There was no objection from the defence camp. Lizzie — with everyone in court trying to imagine what she looked like, trying to match a face with the voice, wondering if she looked anything like Rachel — told how she had become involved with Colin Stagg through a series of letters, phone calls and meetings. As a result she had made 31 different witness statements running into thousands of words, throughout the first six months of 1993. 'And those statements are true?' asked prosecutor Boyce.

'Yes they are, Your Worship,' she replied, addressing the magistrate direct in the customary manner of a trained police officer. That was it. The court was to hear no more, as yet, about that extraordinary six months of her life. The expected revelations of her strange and frightening mock romance with Colin Stagg were to be kept for the Old Bailey jury.

However, before she made her secret exit from court, Mr Sturman wanted to know a few things on behalf of his client, now sitting in the dock an accused man, but once a lovelorn suitor full of sexual anticipation. 'In the course of your normal life, forgetting you are a police officer, has any man ever lied to impress you?' Mr Sturman asked the policewoman. 'Yes, he has,' she admitted, as almost any attractive young woman would be forced to confess, such is the cynicism in romance these days.

'During all your meetings and conversations you were acting as a serving police officer?' — 'I was a serving police officer,' Lizzie replied emphatically, ensuring that no-one was under any illusion that she had been playing a deadly serious role for real, not some theatrical lead in a TV thriller.

'You were trying to see whether Mr Stagg would incriminate himself in the murder of Rachel Nickell?'

'No,' said the voice firmly, sensing that she was being invited to say it was a trap. 'I was trying to find out if he was implicated or not.'

Turning to one of the more bizarre sexual fantasies

she had sent to Stagg as part of the operation, Mr Sturman asked whose imagination had been at work. It was, said Lizzie, a joint effort between herself, Mr Wickerson and Mr Pedder, working within the guidelines set by Mr Britton. And what was her reaction when details of Scotland Yard's most secret undercover operation, and her involvement in it, were splashed all over the daily papers after Stagg's arrest? 'Horrified, Your Worship.'

Just 30 minutes in the witness box and Lizzie was gone. Tension in the courtroom visibly eased. It had been, in fact, little more than an academic exercise. Magistrate Terry English — who had been promoted to circuit court judge during the committal proceedings, to a chorus of congratulations from his legal associates — had already read the mass of transcripts detailing her evidence in order to satisfy himself that it was admissible in court. It took most of his weekend, ploughing through dozens of hardcore sexual fantasies, vile letters, and suggestive tape recordings, for him to form the conclusion that the material was relevant and should go forward to the trial as part of the prosecution case. Without it, the Crown case would have been left desperately thin.

Earlier in the proceedings, Mr Sturman had also submitted that the Britton evidence, with which Lizzie's testimony was inextricably linked, should also be booted out of court. The psychologist's testimony, said the lawyer disparagingly, boiled down to the simple assertion: 'I am Britton, therefore I am right.' But, said Mr Sturman, there was no scientific analysis to explain his conclusions. 'Psychology is a discipline of the mind — there are no facts to back it up,' said Mr Sturman. It was, he argued, evidence that was speculative and unsupported by anything other than Britton's own intuition. Asked how it could be checked, Britton had simply said, 'By other psychologists.' This type of witness could be a 'dangerous type of animal . . . and I don't mean that in a derogatory sense to Mr Britton', said the lawyer.

He claimed a lot of the letters to Stagg were clearly 'come-ons' from Lizzie James, contrived to get Stagg to commit his wildest fantasies to paper. She wrote saying she wanted Stagg to take charge, to show her who was boss. 'You would need to be a moron not to know this was a woman who wanted to be dominated,' he said. It was hardly surprising that Stagg had replied the way he did. Nothing of a violent sado-masochistic nature had been found at his home to back up Mr Britton's analysis . . . just a copy each of soft-porn girlie magazines *Escort* and *Razzle*, fairly ordinary bedside company for a fit and healthy bachelor.

Stagg had written complaining that he was sad and lonely and fed up with people sneering at him in the street. 'They were the letters of a man writing to someone he, sadly, believed to be his friend,' said Mr Sturman. Britton, he said, was a partisan witness and his evidence should not be tolerated, he told the magistrate in an eloquent attempt to persuade him to ban the whole offender profiling package. 'The Crown cannot call this man to give evidence. He has no medical qualifications and he is simply trying to guess Stagg's sexual behaviour. We simply do not know what other lunatic was there on the common that day.'

Mr Britton, argued the lawyer, was simply not

competent to give evidence in a case which was set to make legal history if it was sent to the Old Bailey. His interpretation of Stagg's letters, one of the central parts of the Crown case, 'means that, heads, Stagg loses; tails, Britton wins. In an impassioned plea to the magistrate, Mr Sturman said, 'The Crown seek to make legal history by calling a psychologist's evidence as proof positive of murder. On the basis that Mr Britton's evidence is tentative at best, and this is a clear case where the evidence offends against all principles of fairness and common law, I ask you to exclude it.'

Mr Boyce argued that, as far as the prosecution was concerned, Mr Britton was an eminent and well-respected psychologist of many years' experience and his evidence should be fairly placed alongside any other for a jury to consider. Only then would they have the full picture of an extremely unusual case laid out before them. Only then, with all the evidence fully available, would they be able to make that vital decision on whether Colin Stagg was a merciless killer or a sick victim of his own harmless fantasies. It took Mr English an overnight consideration before announcing, in no-nonsense tones, that he was satisfied the evidence was wholly admissible and what the jury should be concerned with was the weight of it and that they should attach what importance they felt it merited in the overall context of the case.

Undaunted by his two failed attempts to have evidence excluded, Mr Sturman was back on the attack when Detective Inspector Pedder was called to the witness box on the final day of the committal proceedings. 'Did you,' he asked the police officer, 'consult an expert on the pagan religion during inquiries into Stagg's background?' No, said the officer, he didn't personally make inquiries but it was done on behalf of the squad. Did the expert say that, essentially, paganism was a non-violent religion? 'That is my understanding,' said the detective. And is one of the main themes that any harm you do to another person comes back to you multiplied by three? 'That is my understanding, but I'm not sure about the multiplication,' replied the officer.

Had he sought Mr Britton's assistance in interviewing any of the 32 or 33 other suspects who had been questioned? — 'No'. When was Britton consulted about Stagg? — 'It would have been about three days after Mr Stagg was first in custody.' And who was it, asked Mr Sturman, who tipped off the press that Stagg would be appearing at Wimbledon court on an indecent exposure charge after his first arrest, resulting in his picture being plastered all over the papers? 'I assume a statement would have been issued by the Metropolitan Police Press Bureau,' said the officer. What about other lines of inquiry in the murder, inquired Mr Sturman, were they all followed up thoroughly? Jabbing at a bundle of notes in his hands, itemising many thousands of lines of police inquiries, he asked about an inquiry listed as Action 2337 — the sighting of Rachel and Alex talking to a man on a bike on Wimbledon Common in June 1992. There was, recalled the inspector, a report of a man resembling the videofit murder suspect seen talking to a woman and child, but he couldn't be certain they were Rachel and Alex. However, the line of inquiry came to nothing anyway, he said. How many names altogether were offered by the public as fitting the videofit following the Crimewatch programme? asked Mr Sturman — 'quite a lot'. Would the officer agree that Wimbledon Common has more than its fair share of sex pests? — 'I would agree with that,' said the detective who had, out of necessity, become acquainted with the worst of the perverts during the course of the murder investigation.

'Including a substantial number of those with sexual peculiarities, those who masturbate, flash and have sex in the woods?' asked Mr Sturman.

'I don't know about their mental state but, yes, there are,' agreed the detective.

And were there over a hundred people living within a mile of the common who are convicted sex offenders? — 'I wouldn't disagree with that,' he said. Was the officer aware that a man called Curtis was the first to be arrested in connection with the murder? — 'I am aware, although I was not involved at the time.' He fitted the description of the assailant? — 'I wouldn't dispute that.' Was the coroner's assistant's boyfriend warned about revealing Rachel's injuries because it could hinder inquiries? — 'He was certainly spoken to.' Was a decision taken after Stagg's first arrest not to check out any other suspects? — 'No, it wasn't,' said the officer emphatically. 'Other lines of inquiry, including some persons who fitted the videofit, were continued for some months.'

Did he remember, asked the lawyer, about a man seen by police at the Windmill car park on 23 December 1992, who would pass as a twin of Colin Stagg? — 'I have no recollection but I have no doubt that I was informed. I don't know what action was taken.' Who put out a press release saying identification was not an issue in the Stagg case? — 'Again that was an issue for the Metropolitan Police Press Bureau. Having seen the Press Bureau log, it reads "I/D is not an issue". It is the view of the senior investigating officers that the use of the abbreviation 'ID led to the terms "identification" and "identity" being confused. The Met. Police view was that identification was not an issue as no further identity parades could be held because Mr Stagg's picture had been published after he left court on 21 September 1992. Any identification parade would have been evidentially worthless.'

Were bike tracks found at the scene of the murder ever identified? — 'They were, as a type widely used on various types of cycles.' Despite Dr Shepherd being able to do a remarkable reconstruction of the murder weapon, using a liver scan, police had never found the knife? — 'That's correct.' Did the police ever consider showing little Alex a video picture of Stagg? — 'No, I don't think that was ever discussed. I do recall that discussions were held to consider some form of identification procedure in which Alex would be involved.' Was that abandoned because the little boy named somebody? — 'No it wasn't. He did name somebody but it wasn't Stagg.' He named a man some people thought was obsessed with Rachel? — 'Yes, that's correct.' Was Mr Britton asked to profile that man? — 'No'.

So, said Mr Sturman, on the evidence presented so far, it was surely a dangerous case in which to send a man for trial on a charge of murder. He urged Mr English to throw it out, here and now, and let Colin Stagg have his freedom. There was, he said, no forensic evidence to link Stagg with the murder, three eye witnesses on the common had failed to pick him out, Paul Britton's evidence was contradictory and in the Lizzie James operation it was 'blindingly obvious' that the stakes had been deliberately raised by the WPC in an attempt to get Stagg to confess. 'I ask you to pause very carefully before you decide whether or not to commit him for trial,' said Mr Sturman. Stagg, in T-shirt and jeans as usual, looked mildly hopeful as his lawyer sat down.

Mr Boyce, on the other hand, was insistent that there was a strong case to answer. Stagg's alibi of being asleep at the time of the murder had been blown apart, Mrs Harriman's three positive identifications of Stagg were rock solid and Mr Britton had found his behaviour patterns indistinguishable from those of the killer.

Mr English kept no-one in suspense. Like the experienced magistrate he was, he had weighed up the evidence as it went along. 'I don't intend to retire for purely cosmetic reasons,' he said. 'I've had eleven days to consider both arguments — which I had anticipated — and it is my decision this case should be committed for trial at the Central Criminal Court.' It was a legal decision based, of course, on the strength of the evidence he had heard. He chastised Mr Sturman for daring to suggest in his defence submissions that the case had just 'limped' through the committal process, implying that the prosecution was playing a weak hand and that they were somewhat lucky the decision had gone their way.

Ever-optimistic, Jim Sturman thought, nevertheless, that Stagg should at least get bail while he awaited trial. Nobody else believed he had a prayer, given the nature of the charge against him. Detective Inspector Pedder could hardly have been more hostile to such a move. The police objections, he said, were a belief that Stagg might commit further offences, that he would interfere with witnesses, he might abscond before the trial and should certainly be kept in custody for his own safety. The magistrate interjected, 'He is innocent in law. We should not be talking about re-offending.' Pedder pointed out that it was Mr Britton's conclusion that re-offending was almost inevitable if, indeed, his analysis of the situation proved correct. Stagg, said the officer, was still writing to various prosecution witnesses claiming that they were telling lies. These letters were causing concern and the police had had to move at least one witness from her home. Requests for protection had been made by others. One witness had received a phone threat not to give evidence. It was not made by Stagg but was at his instigation. Cheryl Lewis had been threatened by other residents on the Alton Estate and accused of helping the police. Because of Stagg's reclusive lifestyle he had no community ties which would keep him in the area and could easily flee before the trial. Further, the outrage caused by the murder placed him in a position of danger for his personal safety. 'The estate is divided into two camps — those for Mr Stagg and those vehemently against him,' said Pedder.

Mr Sturman said Stagg had made no direct threats but was making contact with various people on the estate to say, in effect, 'I thought you were my friends. Why are you saying these things about me?' These are cries from the heart from a man who has protested his innocence all along and will continue to protest his innocence until the day he dies.' He said Stagg was a man who lived simply with his dog, did not feel threatened and would be happy to stay with a relative outside London until the time came for him to face trial.

Mr English had little hesitation in turning down the bail application because of the gravity of the offence leading to substantial fears that he would not attend his trial. Stagg went back to Wandsworth Prison, ever-loyal mum and stepdad went back home to ponder over the evidence they had heard, and Jim Sturman said again, 'It's going to be a very interesting trial.' It was something of an understatement.

The murder team were able to relax a little. One hurdle was cleared. The toughest part was yet to come. The Old Bailey trial, the experts predicted, could last anything up to eight weeks. The senior police officers involved in the affair had all been down this road many times in previous cases. They knew all too well the vagaries of the British jury system. Nothing was ever a foregone conclusion. Nevertheless, on that miserable, wet February evening, they were confident that they had the right man for Rachel's murder and that they had conducted as thorough and impartial an investigation as was possible in highly exceptional circumstances. Nobody wanted the wrong man jailed. And nobody wanted a guilty man to cheat justice.

Normally the police will relax and open up a little at this stage of a major inquiry, perhaps giving out a few interesting titbits of information which would be useful to curious reporters at the end of the trial. However, there was still extreme caution in the Stagg case — an air of distrust — as the police team sat with their beers in the Alexandra pub, round the corner from the courthouse. Internal inquiries were still going on, jobs were on the line, the whole relationship with the press was in question. Was there something, one crime reporter asked tentatively, that you guys know and we don't that makes you so sure Stagg is your man? They just smiled.

Only a few weeks later they were to receive a potentially devastating blow to their case, which left little room for smiling for many, many months and threw into doubt whether Colin Stagg would ever face a murder trial jury. In another part of Britain, a man facing a murder charge was cleared after a judge ruled that the evidence of an undercover policewoman, acting in a role uncannily like that of Lizzie James, was inadmissible. Mobile grocer Keith Hall walked from court, laughing all over his face, after the judge's ruling led to a jury acquitting him of killing his wife Patricia.

It was a vitally important legal judgment for the Wimbledon detectives and prosecution lawyers, creating a legal precedent which Stagg's defence team would almost certainly cite at the Old Bailey before the start of his murder trial. Lose the evidence of the WPC and they could lose the case, the police feared. There were too many worrying parallels with their investigation.

Like Lizzie James, the undercover officer in the Hall case had befriended Hall through a lonely hearts ad in a newspaper. Like Lizzie James, she had formed a relationship in which the man became utterly besotted. And like Lizzie James her letters, phone calls and hours of conversation were all recorded to form a key part of the prosecution case. Even the name was virtually the same — Liz, short for Eliza. Eliza had been brought in to help the police in West Yorkshire to crack the mystery of Keith Hall's missing wife. Patricia Hall vanished after neighbours had heard a blazing row coming from their home in Moorland Drive, Pudsey, in the spring of 1992. Hall claimed she had stormed out in a huff, taking the family's Ford Sierra car, and disappeared into thin air. The car was later found abandoned, with the driving seat positioned to suit Mrs Hall's size. However, a local milkman recalled seeing someone he thought was a man sitting in the driving seat. Police suspected Hall of murder and dug in the garden of the couple's semi, looking for a body. They also excavated under concrete at a newly-laid roundabout nearby. Hall was questioned but, on his solicitor's advice, said nothing. The police were foxed.

Then, early in October 1992, a Pudsey woman, known only as Eliza, put an ad in the lonely hearts column of the *Wharf Valley Times*. She was amazed to receive a reply from Keith Hall, whose name had been blazoned across newspapers in the area as a result of the investigation into his missing wife. She had been missing only six months and here was Hall looking for a new love. Worried Eliza phoned Pudsey police station and talked to Detective Inspector Jim Bancroft in the incident room. He asked her to write back to Hall to see where it led. Hall replied and told her, 'I want to put some meaning back into my life.'

The police, frustrated that their investigation was getting nowhere, decided to replace Eliza with an undercover policewoman to see what information she could glean about the missing wife. Officer Liz was chosen from the ranks of the West Yorkshire Regional Crime Squad. She had to appeal to Hall physically and emotionally. Liz, who had never worked on an undercover operation before, was picked because she was slightly smaller than Hall's five feet seven inches, was pretty but not glamorous, knew Pudsey well enough to pose as a local and was able to switch into the local Yorkshire dialect, matching Hall's clipped tones. The masquerade led Liz to a blind date meeting with Hall in a pub car park, then to drinks and dinner, an engagement ring and talk of setting up home together. Finally, after four months of pretence, she got what she was after — a confession by Hall that he had murdered his wife, that he had strangled her and burned her body in an incinerator. The damning admission was recorded on a mini-microphone hidden inside WPC Liz's dress, transmitting every word to police 'minders' hiding in a van parked round the corner and containing a sophisticated tape recorder.

The Crown Prosecution Service, which, up to that point, had said there was insufficient evidence to charge Hall, then agreed that the WPC's evidence gave them enough to go ahead. Three days later Hall was arrested, charged and remanded in jail for a year to await his trial. However, at Leeds Crown Court in March 1994, a jury found him not guilty of murder after the judge, Mr Justice Waterhouse, ruled Liz's hardwon evidence to be inadmissible and banned her from testifying. Wimbledon police — who were unaware of the Yorkshire operation — were astonished at the number of similarities with their own inquiry and deeply concerned that their own undercover evidence was now in danger.

Keith Hall walked from court grinning like a Cheshire cat and promptly sold his story to the *News of the World* for a substantial sum. Newspaper ethics about paying criminals were not breached as he was deemed to be an innocent man.

Forgetting any connection with the Rachel Nickell inquiry, the Hall case was fascinating in its own right, raising as it did the moral and ethical issues of such dangerous undercover operations, the potential risks involved and the question of just how far a young policewoman should be expected to go in the pursuit of evidence. No doubt the discussion would be raised again once the Rachel case was over.

However, for now the Wimbledon team had to concentrate their efforts on ensuring that their undercover girl's evidence would not be destined for the legal dustbins. They knew the very foundation of the prosecution case was in danger of being undermined and Keith Pedder decided on an urgent trip to Leeds for a consultation with Detective Inspector Bancroft and a good long look through the files in the Hall case. Somewhere in there, he was certain, was legal ammunition which would save their case from obliteration by some high-powered defence attorney. Although Stagg was now committed for trial the battle was beginning all over again for the squad at Wimbledon police station.

As Hall toasted his freedom in a pub in Leeds his solicitor Rodney Lester was making life uncomfortable for Bancroft and his team. 'My client believes Pudsey police have harassed him,' he said. 'They were like fishermen hooking a fish and using an attractive woman as bait hoping to reel him in.' Wasn't that exactly what

Colin Stagg's solicitors were saying too?

The trial date for Colin Stagg was fixed for September 1994. Stagg's prison visitors found him becoming ever more optimistic about his chances of an acquittal — if, indeed, he ever faced trial at all, for the police and prosecution lawyers were now forced to concede that if Stagg's defence team successfully applied to the trial judge for the evidence of Lizzie James to be disallowed, coupled so closely as it was with that of Paul Britton, then they would be forced to throw in the towel and offer no further evidence. Colin Stagg would be automatically freed, to return as an innocent man to his home, his dog and Wimbledon Common . . . and possibly a newspaper fortune for his story. His mum and stepfather had already started talking deals with newspapers and had received some advance payments 'to buy Colin some comforts in prison'. Both remained unwavering in their belief that he was innocent, but the pressure showed in Mrs Carr's face. Sitting in her comfortable ground-floor flat in Bendemere Road, Putney, near the Oxford and Cambridge boat race course, she said, 'I never believed Colin could do such a thing. We went to see him in prison after he had been arrested and charged and he was behind a glass screen. I looked him straight in the eyes and said, "Colin, did you do it?" He looked straight back at me and said, "No, I wouldn't even hurt a spider." I know it was the first time I had seen him since his father's funeral but I believed him then and I believe him now.'

Stagg had also been receiving encouraging mail from the Alton Estate. The tide of public opinion seemed to have turned in his favour. Stagg — now prisoner PG 2656, HM Prison Wandsworth — told one couple that neighbours had been 'great' and repeated, 'I am not guilty of the murder of Rachel Nickell. I am in the hospital wing so that they can keep an eye on me. They think I may be suicidal.' He told another friend, 'Dear God, Liz, I haven't done anything. Me and Brandy shouldn't be going through all this. That bastard is still out there free, laughing at me.'

Keith Pedder now reflected wryly on the possibilities that might end his long battle of wits against Colin Francis Stagg. His colleagues on the team, impressed at his dedication, the sheer number of man-hours spent and the legal application of his mind, had bought him a small souvenir to serve as a permanent reminder of this unique investigation . . . a painting of a Scottish mountain scene, entitled *Stag at Bay*. The irony was not misplaced. At bay now, but for how long? The police, ever realistic, knew their chances of a conviction were probably now less than 50:50.

Inadmissible Evidence

All eyes swivelled to watch Colin Stagg as he emerged from the cells and stood facing his accusers in the Old Bailey's famous Number One Court. It was just after 10:38 on the morning of 5 September 1994 and Stagg's appearance sent a frisson of anticipation through the building. It was being talked about as the murder trial of the year, a case which touched upon the most fundamental emotions of millions of ordinary people. Stagg, in a chunky-knit green sweater, rather than his usual lightweight T-shirt, looked composed, almost relaxed, as he strode up the steps from the Old Bailey custody cells and took his place in the dock accompanied by a prison officer on either side. Just a few feet away, to his right, sat Andrew and Monica Nickell, preparing to endure the most harrowing ordeal of their lives. Not once did Stagg look their way. He was almost certainly unaware of their presence among the mass of journalists, lawyers and courtroom staff. For their part Andrew and Monica glanced just occasionally towards the dock, betraying little of the inward turmoil they must have felt, calm and dignified as ever as the trial of the man the Crown alleged had slain their beautiful daughter almost 26 months earlier finally began.

The Nickells knew, by now, that this was not destined to be a conventional criminal trial, that it was sure to evoke memories they would rather forget, that the lawyers and the judge and years of accumulated legal wisdom would decide the fate of Colin Stagg as much as any evidence the police could muster in an investigation they knew had been complex in the extreme. What they wanted now was a conclusion to the nightmare that had haunted them since that July day in 1992; the knowledge of who and why that is so vital to help victims' relatives come to terms with tragedy. They had talked with prosecutor John Nutting and with the police officers in the case and knew the difficulties that lay ahead.

Many, many days of legal argument were scheduled — the word on the legal grapevine was at least ten to fourteen days — before they would know whether the man who sat so close to them, slightly higher in his dock seat, in centre-stage position, would even face a jury, let alone know whether he was the man who had killed their Rachel. It had been anticipated that a jury would be empanelled that morning, then told to go home for anything up to a fortnight while the lawyers discussed the vexatious matter of Lizzie James's evidence. On that testimony, coupled with Paul Britton's analysis of Stagg and his alleged sexual characteristics, the case would stand or fall, that was the one certainty. The trial judge, Mr Justice Ognall, prepared the court shorthand writer for a marathon session by telling her sympathetically that if she felt she needed a break at any stage then she only had to ask.

The defence team, led by eminent QC William Clegg and backed by Jim Sturman, had already submitted an outline of their objections to the judge and had quoted the case of Keith Hall in Leeds as a classic legal precedent to their argument, just as the police team had feared. Mr Clegg suggested it would, perhaps, be better if the jury were not sworn in immediately. It could create some air of mystery in their minds if they were to find themselves sworn in, Bible in hand, for one of the most important cases in years, only to be told they must go home for a couple of weeks and sit twiddling their thumbs before being called back to hear the evidence. They would surely wonder what had gone on in their absence. It might be better; he ventured, for the jury to be sworn in fresh on the day the trial proper was due to start and for them not to be concerned with any mysterious legalities which may have occurred in their absence.

The judge said that that seemed like the best idea and ruled that the jury should not take their seats until the legal arguments had been concluded and his judgment duly delivered on the crucial matter of Lizzie James's astonishing undercover operation. That, of course, meant that the judge himself would need to familiarise himself with all the material, all those hundreds of pages of evidence, which had been gleaned from Lizzie James's covert courtship with Colin Stagg. It was a monumental task which clearly could not be achieved by even the swiftest of readers or the most agile of legal minds in less than a couple of days. The judge set himself three days, to be on the safe side, to sit at his desk and plough through the transcripts of the bundles of letters that had passed between Stagg and Lizzie, the tape-recorded meetings and the many phone calls. Only then, he told the prosecution and defence teams, would he be sufficiently well briefed to hear their arguments for and against the admissibility of this essential section of the Crown case.

Mike Wickerson and Keith Pedder sat in court below the judge and just in front of prosecutor Nutting, knowing that this was not just another case in their long careers but a personal and legal milestone, a case certain to provoke widespread repercussions whatever the eventual outcome. They were satisfied that they could have done no more for Rachel Nickell and her family. The banks of hard-back files pigeonholed in blocks of six beside the lawyers — at least 36 at a quick count — and the four metal cabinets on top of the courtroom desk, filled with yet more documents, bore witness to the thoroughness of the police investigation.

Already the press were digging for background stories and the rumours were sweeping the pack. Had Andre Hanscombe really got a new girlfriend in France?

Had he fallen out with Andrew and Monica Nickell over it? Was he over in England for the case? How was little Alex now, more than two years on in a young life that had been so shattered by tragedy? And what about Lizzie James? Would she be permitted by her Scotland Yard bosses to tell her own inside story of her extraordinary role in the Stagg saga? It was a story everyone was anxious to hear, be it in the witness box or outside.

On day one, Hilda and David Carr were conspicuous by their absence in the packed public gallery, overlooking the courtroom like the 'gods' in a Victorian theatre. Every seat was taken as Stagg glanced quickly upwards, then away, without apparently recognising anyone. By now he had built up a small army of supporters who were utterly convinced of his innocence. Several had written to him in Wandsworth Prison, sending messages of good luck and small gifts. Stagg would write back saying how he was looking forward to his freedom, anxious to be reunited with his beloved Brandy and keen to resume tending his now overgrown garden. One of them, Alton Estate neighbour Mrs Lee Brooking, had even sent him new shirts for his Old Bailey appearance. She had met him after his first arrest and had kept in contact ever since. She said Stagg had told her that he was totally innocent and that he had become the 'second innocent victim' of the man who really killed Rachel Nickell. She feared he would kill himself in prison if he was convicted. Now, however, as the lawyers went back to their chambers and the journalists to the pub after the unexpected court adjournment, he was far from suicidal.

On the second day of the hearing, Thursday 8 September, Hilda and David Carr were among the first to arrive at court. They queued outside the Old Bailey's public entrance to await the opening of the doors at 10.30 a.m. then walked up the stairs to take their seats in the front of the public gallery, looking directly down on the dock and peering anxiously at the steps where Colin would come up from the cells. For Hilda it was another painful reminder of family problems past and present and the stress told on her face. She had seen Tony and Lee in trouble already, and now here was Colin, the quiet one, facing a terrible murder charge.

Mr Clegg got straight to the point in the no-nonsense manner which had seen him become one of Britain's most sought-after defence lawyers. This police operation, he said, was a sophisticated 'sting' set up by the police to trick a confession out of Colin Stagg and should not be allowed in evidence. He wanted all the Lizzie James testimony thrown out and all the hand-in-glove psychological evidence which went with it to be deemed inadmissible as well. He knew the matter would be fresh in Mr Justice Ognall's mind after 48 hours of solid reading, of ploughing studiously through more than 700 pages of evidence, much in the outer realms of depravity, that were now the subject of this cornerstone debate. He also knew that if he won the legal battle and the judge ruled in his favour then he was on the threshold of a notable victory. It was generally accepted in both camps that without the Lizzie James evidence, coupled with that of Paul Britton, the prosecution case would be so weakened that they would have little alternative but to offer no further evidence and allow Stagg to be discharged.

Mr Clegg ran through the details of the murder in

brief outline. How Rachel had met her end on a summer day as she strolled with Alex and Molly; how, of the 500 people known to have been on the common that day all but four had since been traced; and how, of the 30-odd men questioned about the killing Colin Stagg had been the one eventually charged. He had always denied any involvement and had originally been freed after three days of questioning because the police had insufficient evidence.

Then came the Lizzie James undercover operation, designed, he said, to trap Stagg into making a confession, taking advantage, he suggested, of a lonely and vulnerable young man's desperate desire to form a relationship with a woman. And, he said, there had also been inducements of money, small amounts admittedly, when Stagg was known to be so short of ready cash that he couldn't find enough for a bus fare. Mr Clegg sought to begin proving his argument by starting right at the beginning of Operation Edzell, with the very first letter penned by Lizzie early in January 1993, for court purposes labelled exhibit EJ1.

The judge appeared slightly alarmed that Mr Clegg was preparing to wade through the entire bundle of Lizzie evidence in support of his submissions. Please read as much as you like, the judge told him tactfully, but he would not advocate reciting the lot and would leave it to Mr Clegg's discretion. 'I certainly don't intend to read all 700 pages,' the defence lawyer quickly assured the judge, but some parts were vitally important to the defence case, he said, and must be given an airing in front of His Lordship and the court. For example, the very first introductory letter in which Lizzie described her supposed friend Julie Pines as 'a little old-fashioned in her attitude if you know what I mean'. It was a clear 'come-on' from the start, he argued, and got worse as the relationship progressed.

Lizzie described herself excitingly as an attractive blonde aged 30 whose favourite record was 'Walk on the Wild Side' by Lou Reed. This grabbed unsuspecting Stagg's interest straight away and he put pen to paper the very same day to reply, telling this new-found friend that he was sometimes painfully lonely and liked to relax by walking his dog and occasionally sunbathing naked.

By the third letter, suggested Mr Clegg, Lizzie began turning up the heat emotionally by saying she hadn't had a relationship with a man for a very long time and longed for the company 'that only a man can give'. It was a 'very deliberate sexual undertone' to lead Stagg on, claimed the defence lawyer. It clearly implied, he said, that here was someone who was ready to become a sexual partner.

Stagg wrote back saying he'd never had a sex life but thrived on sexual fantasies, an example of which he enclosed, detailing his longings for sex in the open air in the garden. Lizzie James's response was to send Stagg a Valentine card in which she wrote light-heartedly, 'Roses are red, violets are blue, there will be a letter, arriving for you. Guess who?' and signed with a kiss. Now Lizzie was 'very obviously' trying to shape the course of the relationship, complained Mr Clegg, by portraying herself as someone sexually experienced, ready, willing and able, knowing full well that Stagg was a virgin and desperate to lose that tag. In reply to one of his fantasy letters she had told him, 'It was so real I could almost feel you sitting astride me, pushing me into the ground.' She praised his brilliant story telling and urged him to write more fantasies.

Mr Clegg told the judge: 'This officer was clearly encouraging him to write more extreme fantasies, controlling the relationship and setting the pace of the future contact.' A photograph from Lizzie — given pride of place on his mantelpiece — sent him into raptures and he told her 'you are very beautiful . . . I can't wait to feel your warm lips against me . . . You look like a very passionate woman.' He confessed that he had never been attractive to women and had 'all the fantasies inside me, unused'. Lizzie wrote back, urging Stagg to go further and further with his letters, said Mr Clegg, by saying her imagination knew no bounds and 'normal' things were not enough for her. Quite clearly, said Mr Clegg, she was trying to make Stagg believe she had uninhibited deviant fantasies, in a bid to get him to respond with even more lurid stories of his own which might be relevant to the Rachel murder inquiry.

Sometimes, said Mr Clegg, the WPC would deliberately not reply to Stagg, to keep him in suspense. 'We detect,' he said, 'that when the fantasies do not progress as the officer wishes there is no reply, but when the fantasies increase in intensity, she replies swiftly with more encouragement.' She tried to prise more detail out of him, suggested the lawyer, by saying that there were secrets they must share with each other before they can be 'together for ever'.

The judge interjected, 'This is a springboard to saying that before there could be a union between us two you must unburden your innermost thoughts.' Mr

Clegg agreed that that was exactly his point — that Lizzie was dangling the carrot of romance and sex before Stagg in the hope of a revealing confession in return.

The policewoman, he suggested, became more and more frustrated with Stagg when he failed to produce what she wanted and finally told him she had once taken part in the ritual slaying of a woman and the murder of a child by throat cutting, 'bringing together the woman and child elements of the Rachel Nickell murder'. After the satanic killing, she said she had enjoyed the best sex ever, using the phrase 'it really buzzed'. Stagg then confessed to her of a homosexual relationship at the age of seventeen when he took part in mutual masturbation with another man, but, compared with Lizzie's allegedly turbulent past, this was relatively unexciting. 'It must have been very tame,' said Mr Clegg, 'and it infuriated the WPC. She had hoped he might say, "I killed Rachel Nickell".' But he didn't. Stagg's reply was to claim he had taken part in a completely fictitious murder in the New Forest. 'By confessing to a murder that never happened, the police plan was not working,' said Mr Clegg, with added emphasis. 'So the officer said she wishes he had done the Wimbledon Common murder. But Stagg said, "I'm terribly sorry but I didn't".' The whole operation, argued Mr Clegg, had produced unreliable evidence which should not be admitted in fairness to Colin Stagg. It was, he said, misconceived from inception and it was 'difficult to imagine an operation more calculated to result in material which a court would inevitably withhold as inadmissible. It flies in the face of the rule of self-incrimination . . . one of the fundamental rules of the criminal justice system.'

The judge added, 'That is the right not to incriminate himself without knowing who is the inquisitor.'

It was indeed, agreed Mr Clegg. The undercover operation, claimed Mr Clegg, had precious little safeguard for an innocent man.

Stagg and the officer had talked about the Rachel Nickell murder and Stagg said Rachel had been raped and that is why police took DNA samples from him. Lizzie said the police were certain to get their man. Stagg told her they couldn't take samples from every man in Britain. The conversation was significant, said Stagg's defender; because Rachel had not been raped and the real killer would have known that.

Stagg listened intently as his lawyer quoted the legal precedents in support of his argument, from weighty judgments by some of Britain's greatest legal minds: Lords Scarman, Goddard, Parker, Widgery and Diplock. The lawyers were in their element. Then it was back to the basics which mere mortals could understand . . . had Lizzie strayed outside the legal parameters to trick Colin Stagg? The policewoman, stormed Mr Clegg, had used lies, promises and blandishments to get her evidence, even suggesting it would be 'great' if Stagg was the Rachel killer. If he had said, 'Yes, it was me', it would be a reliable confession — 'but I can't think of more unreliable circumstances'.

Mr Justice Ognall readily agreed that, in such circumstances, he would have no choice but to disallow such a confession. However, what the Crown now said was that because there was no actual admission they could use the evidence.

Lizzie James, said Mr Clegg, had called the shots in

the relationship and was effectively telling Stagg what she wanted him to write in his fantasy letters. The defence, he said, would be submitting a cassette tape which Lizzie James had sent to Stagg 'containing the most hardcore pornography imaginable'. He told the judge disapprovingly, 'It is happily without precedent and is frankly a disgrace. It is the most extraordinary document for a serving police officer to send a suspect.' He assured the judge he did not intend to read a transcript of the contents. The tape, which Stagg received in June 1993, had apparently been sent by Lizzie after first being cleared by Paul Britton and compiled with the assistance of senior officers. 'It is our submission,' said Mr Clegg 'that this officer, Lizzie James, subjected Stagg to quite deliberate manipulation, designed to get him to incriminate himself.'

He quoted one particular letter which Stagg began by calling the WPC: 'My dear, beautiful, sexy Lizzie' and saying that he now knew the sort of things 'you want me to write'. The officer also offered to lend him money — which he declined — but it showed how far she was prepared to go to get him in her debt, Mr Clegg submitted. She used phrases like 'We might not be right for each other . . . I've been so disappointed in other men,' and 'If you fit my criteria there is no going back and we will be together for ever,' in apparent attempts to prompt Stagg into making a confession about Rachel Nickell. This was trickery, he said and, in the interests of fair play, should never be put before a jury.

There was indeed an element of subterfuge, admitted prosecutor Nutting. But this was a necessarily clandestine operation and was often difficult and dangerous work. What could be used in evidence as a result of such an operation, he accepted, could also be a difficult decision to make. But each case must be judged on its own merits, with the final discretion in the hands of the trial judge. Paul Britton, he said, had masterminded the operation following his offender profiling of the killer from evidence at the scene of the murder. It was different from other operations, he said, because it was not set up to trap or trick Stagg into making a confession but to investigate his sexual fantasies. There would come a time, Britton had predicted, where fantasy and reality would merge and he would discuss the killing. The operation was controlled and interpreted by Britton at all stages and was designed to give Stagg the opportunity to display his innocence if he was not connected with the Rachel murder. Britton controlled each step on the ladder and if, at any stage, Stagg was not following the predicted path the operation would have been stopped.

The police could have stopped the operation at any time they chose, interjected the judge. Were they trying to say they would achieve by the back door what they couldn't by the front door? It was, agreed Mr Nutting, outside the normal realms of police investigations.

His Lordship added, 'The fact that it was being done with a psychologist as puppet master is a vital distinction of principle.'

Mr Nutting agreed and said it underlined the fundamental safeguards programmed into the operation. 'In my submission,' he said 'the evidence-gathering nature of this operation is best illustrated as having value only if interpreted by someone else, rather like a fingerprint obtained by a police officer only has value if evaluated by someone else.' The police, he said, decided to embark on the operation in conjunction with Mr Britton because of the gravity of the crime and the public concern it had aroused. It was sometimes good sense and good law to use alternative methods of investigation when need called. The Lizzie operation was a trick and was deceit, he admitted. But, in cases of really serious crime, courts have come to regard that such methods can serve the purpose of obtaining evidence and attempting to obtain the truth of matters. It was necessary for Lizzie James to have played the role she did because Stagg would certainly never have revealed his fantasies to a normal woman. That, he told the judge, was why the 'sting' had to be perpetrated. The red-robed Mr Justice Ognall, among Britain's most senior judges, with a reputation for being tough but fair, remarked on the striking similarities between the Keith Hall case in Leeds and the Lizzie James operation and awaited Mr Nutting's observations on the matter.

By the end of the second day of legal debate it was becoming apparent that the predicted ten to fourteen days of argument would be very substantially curtailed, probably ending after three or four. The betting was on the case collapsing early the following week. If that were to happen — and Old Bailey experts have very often found themselves on the wrong side of a judge's ruling — then Stagg could be a free man without ever standing trial. As the jury had never been sworn in and the trial never officially started, it would have to be a discharge by the judge, rather than an acquittal by 'twelve men good and true'. The defence team oozed confidence as they sipped Michelob beer at £1.95p a bottle in a wine bar near the Old Bailey that evening. The ever-affable and courteous John Nutting, asked which way he would bet on the judge's ruling, shrugged, smiled and said, 'I wouldn't put any money on me . . .'

It was getting near the time when Colin Stagg would know his fate and the police team would know if their inspirational Operation Edzell and its brave leading lady would, after all, be written off as a calamity under the withering attack of Colin Stagg's lawyers. It might be in the lofty precision of legal judgments, but never among the team who had been there in the front line.

Friday saw the third full day of legal argument in Court One, with the world outside still knowing nothing of the tense drama being played out in the most famous courtroom in the land. Mr Justice Ognall had imposed a reporting ban on the proceedings under section 4(2) of the Contempt Act 1981, designed to prevent the risk of prejudice — in this case the chance of jurors hearing controversial evidence which would not later be used in the event of a full trial. Andrew and Monica Nickell were in court again to hear John Nutting resume the case for allowing the Lizzie James evidence. The law, he said, allowed police undercover operations where they were deemed necessary to obtain evidence where no other methods were available or practical. There was deceit, he said, but it was necessary for the WPC's cover and to assist in building up a psychological profile of a suspect and it had not been conducted for the sole purpose of extracting a confession.

What's the difference, the judge probed, between police using deceit to obtain, say, a blood sample or fingerprint? It was, said Mr Nutting, the fact that the final analysis was always carried out by a third party, in this case Paul Britton. This was, indeed, new ground agreed judge, defence and prosecution, and a new chapter in the history of crime investigation, in which the judge's decision was to have far-reaching consequences — as had Mr Justice Waterhouse's ruling in the Keith Hall case in Leeds, which now threw its shadow over the police case here. Not every trick or deceit is inherently unfair, Mr Nutting ventured. Stagg would only have felt able to reveal his innermost thoughts to Lizzie James because her guise had persuaded him he could trust her. The operation could not have been carried out without some element of deceit and at no stage, he argued, had Lizzie deliberately manipulated Colin Stagg. He wasn't induced to write fantasy letters for the first time — he was already involved in fantasy creations with Julie Pines and appeared to be 'something of a compulsive fantasy writer'. If he hadn't been writing to Lizzie James, said Mr Nutting, he would surely have been writing to someone else.

The judge, not for the first time, gave clear indications to all that he was far from happy with Lizzie James's role. If she had 'seduced or manipulated' Stagg into writing fantasy sex letters 'that creates problems'. The dismay showed on the faces of the police team.

What Lizzie was doing, suggested Mr Nutting in a bid to bolster the flagging prosecution case, was simply creating an atmosphere of trust in which Stagg would have felt safe to reveal his darkest thoughts. He could not have penned his desires about knives and bloodletting to just any woman. Lizzie's cover was vital to the success of the operation, he said. 'She had to be a credible and sympathetic listener to anything he wanted to say, someone committed to a similar cause.' Stagg, he maintained, had been suspicious, fearing it was a journalist's trick, and she was obliged to convince him otherwise.

John Bassett, the police chief who originally headed the investigation, and has now begun a second career with the Federation Against Copyright Theft, made an appearance in court midway through the morning's hearing. During a fifteen-minute break in proceedings, he shook hands warmly with Mr and Mrs Nickell. A few minutes later they could be seen walking slowly, hand in hand, across the great domed hall of the Old Bailey, beneath Gerald Moira's magnificent painted ceiling, comforting each other, as close as husband and wife could ever be.

Back in court, Mr Nutting continued his defence of police tactics by refuting suggestions that Lizzie had incited Stagg to delve into the deviant world of pain and pleasure. It was always Stagg, he insisted, who had made the first moves. One example was him writing: 'I am going to make sure you are screaming when I abuse you . . .' Another was: 'I fuck you hard, my cock ramming into you, pushing you along the ground'. He talked of cutting Lizzie on her neck and breasts with a knife, drawing blood which runs down her body.

'Nothing said by Lizzie James shaped this fantasy,' he stated. The nearest she had got to mentioning any kind of violence was to tell Stagg she enjoyed the leather belt schoolgirl fantasy he had sent her.

The next few minutes in that courtroom must have been almost unendurable for Mr and Mrs Nickell. It was Lizzie's account of Stagg's reaction when he eventually began talking about Rachel and his arrest as a suspect. Mr Nutting said Stagg told her the police had shown him a photograph of her body. 'There was blood all over the grass and she was completely naked,' said Stagg. 'As they showed me the photograph I got a hard on.' He told her he used to go over the common to masturbate afterwards, '. . . but it's a bit dodgy now, the police keep hanging about hoping the murderer will come back'.

Lizzie said, 'I wonder if he does.'

There was more talk about the murder and Lizzie, in an attempt to get him to open up even more, said, 'I wish you had done it and got away with it, that would be brilliant.' Stagg told her he was on the common at the time — which, said Mr Nutting, was different from what he had already told the police. Stagg had also allegedly shown Lizzie how Rachel's hands were clasped, 'as if in prayer' beside her head when she was discovered dead on the common. He gave her a demonstration — later to be copied on video by the policewoman — at one of their meetings in Hyde Park in July 1993, said Mr Nutting. The prosecution leader submitted that only the killer would have known the exact position of Rachel's hands and Stagg's demonstration was capable of being an admission and should be permitted as evidence. It was not something, said Mr Nutting, that Stagg could have seen in the one police picture he had been shown. 'This was a small and insignificant detail to the defendant,' said Mr Nutting, 'which slipped out unintentionally because he forgot to differentiate between what he had seen legitimately in the police picture and what he had seen illegitimately as the murderer.'

Not surprisingly, Mr Clegg rejected all Mr Nutting's

claims over the validity of the Lizzie evidence and offender profiling 'root and branch'. There was, he maintained, absolutely no history of offender profiling ever being used as a principal plank of a prosecution case in British law. In America, in seventeen cases where it had been permitted, all had subsequently been quashed on appeal. 'We say Lizzie James was leading Stagg by the nose,' he said. Her evidence should be despatched in exactly the same way as the undercover evidence in the Leeds case of Keith Hall. 'Hall cannot be distinguished from the facts in this case,' said Mr Clegg.

It was indeed a profoundly important ruling that Mr Justice Ognall was set to make a decision which would cause the police to rethink any future use of offender profiling as a prosecution weapon rather than just an accessory to an investigation. That evening the defence team, Mr Clegg, Jim Sturman, Ian Ryan and their legal staff were drinking champagne in the wine bar just across the road from the Old Bailey. 'It's someone's birthday,' they said.

As court resumed on the following Monday the defence team launched their most devastating attack so far; with Mr Clegg slamming the police undercover operation from beginning to end. From the moment the policewoman described her so-called friend Julie Pines as 'prudish' in her very first letter, she was leading Stagg on, he suggested, expanding a little on his earlier points as he made his final address to Mr Justice Ognall. 'If I had strings to my bow this would be the first,' he said, then added impishly 'or should I say the steps to my ladder', using Paul Britton's often-repeated description for the undercover operation which was now being so roundly rubbished. Lizzie James, far from being a passive partner in this strange romance, had deliberately planted the seeds for Stagg's erotic fantasies, including the scarcely veiled references to Satanism, knives, domination, buggery and violence . . . matters which the police knew were already contained in Paul Britton's offender profile of the killer. Stagg, he suggested, was being encouraged, blackmailed and bribed into incriminating himself to fit that profile. He cited passage after passage from the letters and conversations which passed between the two participants. 'Normal things are not enough' was an open invitation from Lizzie for Stagg to create wilder and more sadistic fantasies and would plant in his mind the idea of anal sex. 'You really took charge at our first meeting,' hinted at her love of domination. She repeatedly held out the promise of sex if he fulfilled her wishes and wrote her more explicit and salacious letters. And she held over him the 'very powerful inducement' that once both of them had unburdened their dark secrets then Stagg would get what he most yearned for — a loving and lasting relationship with a beautiful woman. Lizzie said things like 'I need you to sort me out,' and Stagg repeated the theme in his reply. It was Lizzie who introduced suggestions of the occult and black magic into the relationship when she talked of once being involved in some sort of satanic ritual. It failed to extract from Colin Stagg what the police wanted — a full confession to the Wimbledon murder.

Three months into the operation, suggested Mr Clegg, the police were getting jittery about the lack of progress. Paul Britton had predicted that if Stagg really was their man they would get a result within sixteen weeks. It wasn't happening so the police decided to change tactics. They moved to Lizzie having direct contact with Stagg by phone, not just writing letters and hoping for a revealing fantasy among them. Stagg was, of course, unaware that the calls were being bugged by Scotland Yard's specialist surveillance unit, known as SO10, who were assisting Wimbledon police in the covert operation. Lizzie immediately stepped up the incentive by suggesting that she was ready to go on holiday with Stagg. 'This was a particularly powerful inducement to a man who had never been on holiday with a pretty woman,' said Mr Clegg. Stagg's letters clearly picked up key words that Lizzie had suggested to him, said Mr Clegg, including suggestions that he would spank her while she was dressed in a schoolgirl's or nurse's uniform. But that was not what Lizzie was aiming for and she was getting impatient, he claimed. She tried to prompt more extreme letters by pretending to lose interest in Stagg, and by urging him to match her own bizarre and brutal experiences.

'In our submission,' Mr Clegg told the judge, 'police had gone a long way down this road and it was still going very slowly. Lizzie James gave Stagg powerful hints that he must come up with something stronger if he was to pass muster.' Stagg still didn't respond as the police had hoped so Lizzie James then uttered what had become the pivotal sentence on which the Crown case now seemed to balance . . . 'Frankly, Colin, it wouldn't matter if you had murdered her. I wish you had. It would make it easier for me. I've got something to tell you.' This, said Mr Clegg, was direct encouragement to Stagg and prompted him to write the knife-point sex fantasy which followed soon after and on which the prosecution relied as firm evidence of his sexual deviancy. 'She was saying she didn't care if his was the hand that wielded the knife that killed Rachel Nickell. He was being pushed down the Britton road,' complained Mr Clegg.

Lizzie had tried to stimulate a reaction from Stagg with her satanic slaying story, said the defence lawyer; including in it gory details of how she had held a knife at the victim's throat and drawn it across, spilling blood which she and others involved in the ritual had drunk. It was followed by a full-scale orgy with 'mind blowing' sex. Stagg's response, said Mr Clegg, had been just the opposite to what the police wanted. He told Lizzie the killing was awful, 'especially the baby'. In a desperate last gamble to elicit a confession out of Stagg, said Mr Clegg, Lizzie James told him their relationship would have to end because he had become a disappointment to her. However, the threats, promises and inducements still failed to produce what the police were looking for.

It was at this point that the judge gave his clearest indication to date that he too was unhappy with basic aspects of the police operation. 'I regard the view that Lizzie James was only a listener as untenable,' he said. There were knowing glances among the lawyers and journalists in court. It was a clear indication of the way the judge was thinking. Stagg's freedom now looked assured. During another brief break in proceedings a few minutes later, Jim Sturman sought to have a brief word with Stagg in the cells. The prison officer on dock duty adamantly refused to allow him down. 'Just a second, that's all I need,' implored the lawyer. The dock officer remained implacable. Mr Sturman, clearly unhappy at being denied access to his client, had to be content with a ten-second chat with Stagg over the rails of the dock when the court resumed. Stagg's demeanour revealed little of what had been so important.

Mr Clegg went straight back on the attack. The police, he said, had put pressure on a man who by now, faced with losing the woman he loved, had become depressed and lonely. He came up with the New Forest murder story in an attempt to appease Lizzie James and keep the relationship intact. But his story of killing a twelve-year-old girl by strangulation when he was a youngster was sneered at by Lizzie James, said Mr Clegg. She said at their next meeting, again in Hyde Park, that it was 'just a childish murder' in what was clearly another bid to extract a bigger and better confession. She told Stagg she could still recall the sound of the knife going in during the ritual slaying and said they needed a 'common bond' if they were to stay together. Again, there was no response.

Then came the extraordinary fantasy tape that Lizzie sent Stagg in an attempt to move things along. 'I've read the transcript of this more than once,' said Mr Justice Ognall, as if the matter troubled him deeply. Mr Clegg assured His Lordship yet again that he wasn't planning to read the transcript in open court, but that he felt it should be made clear that it was in this fantasy that the undercover policewoman has Stagg holding a knife during sex. Any suggestion of Stagg becoming sexually aroused over the thought of the Rachel Nickell killing, said Mr Clegg, was simply because he was trying to match the height of emotion supposedly experienced by Lizzie during her satanic ritual. Lizzie James was, at all stages in the operation, suggested Mr Clegg, directly or indirectly interrogating Stagg 'to all intent and purpose'. He submitted that it was impossible to separate any individual parts of the evidence — 'All the transcripts are either admissible or inadmissible,' he said, 'in order to explain to a jury the history of the relationship, the lies, the encouragements, her shaping of events, her withdrawals and the way Stagg picked up on her suggestions and reproduced them himself. It is all or nothing.' And that, of course, included every word from Paul Britton as well. Mr Clegg's submissions were over. He put down his notes and took his seat. The operation which had looked so promising back in 1993 now looked fragile under his clinical dissection.

It was exactly 12:30 on the dot as the judge announced that his ruling would be made two days later, on the Wednesday. A silence descended on the courtroom as Mr Justice Ognall collected his papers together; nodded towards the assembled lawyers then said, 'Ten-thirty Wednesday. If not then, two p.m.' Colin Stagg could be home by lunchtime. However, what he wanted most of all was just to be reunited with his old mate Brandy.

At one stage, Stagg had gone on hunger strike in Wandsworth Prison after hearing reports that Brandy was seriously ill with liver problems and having been refused permission to visit the dog. His concern was unnecessary — the report was untrue. In fact Brandy was in good care at a boarding kennels in Windsor, Berkshire, fit, healthy and no doubt looking forward to his romps on the common again.

There was no such happy anticipation among the

police team. Mike Wickerson gave a dejected thumbs down to a police colleague as he left court. Keith Pedder looked disappointed. However, both men were professionals. You win some, you lose some, but losing this one was going to be particularly hard. It had been a long and difficult road but, whatever happened in the next few days, they were sure it had been the right thing to do for Rachel and her boy. They would have liked a jury of ordinary folk to have had the opportunity to decide for themselves and not have lawyers pull the carpet from under their feet at this early stage. Still, the law of the land is all-important in these matters. From every inquiry that goes wrong you learn a little for the ones ahead.

Detective Constable Roger Lane, for instance, had emerged from the investigation as a police expert on the Wicca religion. For a down-to-earth, pipe-smoking London copper it had been a strange journey into the world of witchcraft, high priestesses, mystical gods and naked worship. It also sparked off a fascination in the subject in his sixteen-year-old schoolgirl daughter Claire, which resulted in her writing a much-praised essay entitled 'An Insight into Wicca' illustrated with a picture of naked witches in a Cornish coven performing a ritual to invoke the spirit of the mythical Owlman and cloaked figures performing moonlight ceremonies in a magic circle. Claire wrote:

> In country fields, city flats and suburban back gardens men and women meet to raise energy and put themselves in tune with nature. Witches believe that there is much to be learnt by studying

the past, through myth, ritual drama, poetry and song and by living in harmony with the earth and its fellow creatures . . . Witches like to worship "skyclad" — that is without clothes — as they feel it is the way in which they can get closest to nature. But people can be offended by this and they develop an opinion that Wicca is just an excuse for an orgy . . . Spell casting is usually carried out at the esbats as it is believed that the moon influences psychic powers and these are strongest at full moon. Witches believe that magic will rebound so they are careful to practise only in a positive light.

Claire, whose school is at Reigate in Surrey, researched the Wicca festivals of Samhain, Yule, Candlemas, Ostara, Beltane and Lammas and talked to a coven's high priestess. 'The priests and priestesses of Wicca are very strict about who joins the coven because there are many who want to join for the wrong reason,' she wrote. 'People who are interested in Wicca for its sexual content are made aware that Wiccans see sex in the positive rather than the negative light. Rape, child abuse, ritual mutilation and other forms of sexual coercion of which witches are often accused by the media and those with over-active imagination form no part of Wiccan ethics.' Her refreshing assessment of the 'crafte', free of the cynicism of journalists and suspicions of police officers, concludes: 'Wicca is a religion that never seeks to harm others or to practise black magic, otherwise known as Satanism. It is sad that even today witches have to keep their religion secret in order to maintain a life without prejudice.' There are, believes Claire, some 250,000 practising witches in Britain today.

Where did Colin Stagg, self-confessed pagan, fit into this alternative world now as he sat in his prison cell counting the hours until freedom?

'Where's the Justice?'

Dark clouds were whipping rain across London as Colin Stagg made what was to be his final journey to the Old Bailey from Wandsworth Prison. It was nothing to the storm that was to burst over the Rachel Nickell case by the end of the day. As Stagg arrived, the court was already under siege from the biggest media circus seen in years at a criminal trial. The tension was tangible as TV crews set up cameras in the street, photographers pushed for pitches outside the main doors and reporters clustered early inside Court Number One — so many of them that they spilled into the seats normally used by the jury and spread through the rows of public seats at the back. Andrew and Monica Nickell were in their usual seats to the right of the dock as the usher called, 'Silence and be upstanding' and Mr Justice Ognall emerged in a swirl of red robes to take his seat. Following him came an American judge and his wife, on a visit to England from California and now about to witness the highest level of judicial drama likely to be seen anywhere in the world as they sat beside His Lordship.

Stagg's family had gathered in strength up in the gallery. Stagg himself, in black shirt and blue jeans, gave a quick look round the packed court and then fixed his eyes on Mr Justice Ognall. The judge surveyed the ranks of newspaper reporters with pens poised, the TV and radio journalists with clipboard notepads, and suspected there could be a mad scamper for telephones once he had started his judgment. 'I want no unseemly to-ing and fro-ing while I am talking,' he said sternly. 'If any of you want to leave you should do so now.' Not a soul moved.

He began reading from the ruling that was destined to become legal history. The police and the prosecution team knew quickly that their cause was lost but never in their worst nightmares had they imagined the damning indictment that was to follow. The police operation with Lizzie James was, said Mr Justice Ognall, 'thoroughly reprehensible'. He went on:

'I would be the first to acknowledge the pressures on police but I'm afraid this behaviour betrays not merely an excess of zeal but a blatant attempt to incriminate a suspect by positive and deceptive conduct of the grossest kind. A careful appraisal of the material demonstrates a skilful and sustained enterprise to manipulate the accused, sometimes subtly, sometimes blatantly, and designed, by deception, to manoeuvre and seduce him to reveal fantasies of an incriminating character and to, wholly unsuccessfully, admit the offence. The prosecution said the undercover operation was the only route open to them. Well, if a police operation involves the clear trespass into impropriety the court must stand firm and bar the way.'

The judge was particularly scathing over the tape recording sent by Lizzie to Stagg, containing what had been called hardcore pornography, and he now openly voiced the criticism he had implied during the days of legal arguments. The sending of the sex tape, he said, was 'thoroughly reprehensible' and added, 'I would be the first to acknowledge the great pressure on officers in the pursuit of this inquiry but this behaviour was excessive.' In her letters, he said, Lizzie James had used what were to become known as 'honey pot' bribes of sex and love to persuade him to write the kind of fantasies she wanted to hear. The early fantasy letters from Stagg, he said, were the not unusual — if rarely expressed — yearnings of a young heterosexual male but Stagg was clearly pressured by promises of sex and a lasting, loving relationship into creating more exaggerated fantasies of an incriminating nature. Lizzie, he said, had played on the emotions of a lonely and vulnerable man. 'The policewoman was acting under orders and the police, in turn, were being guided by the psychologist, but that cannot excuse the instigation of this sort of strategy.'

The murder of Rachel Nickell, he said, had been a 'truly terrible' crime. 'Any legitimate steps taken by the police and the prosecuting authorities to bring the perpetrator to justice are to be applauded, but the emphasis must be on the word "legitimate".' He called into question the use of psychology in such an investigation and said, 'I would not want to wish to give encouragement to officers to construct, or seek to supplement, investigations of this kind on this basis.'

Despite the 'powerful incentives' offered by Lizzie, Stagg had consistently denied murdering Rachel Nickell. He had been detained first for three days, had answered all questions put to him and had provided an alibi. He even invented a murder which never happened in a bid to placate Lizzie. The judge disputed the prosecution claim that the purpose of the undercover operation was either to elicit evidence from Stagg or to eliminate him from inquiries. He said, 'I believe it was not merely anticipated, but intended, that there should be, eventually, incriminating evidence from the mouth of the suspect. It is very important to my mind that at no stage did the accused ever admit that he was the murderer. Indeed, to the contrary, he repeatedly denied it.' Even when, latterly, he was invited by Lizzie James to admit the crime as a condition of continuing a liaison that he was manifestly desperate to maintain at all costs, he said he was innocent of the offence. On two occasions, he said, Stagg had given details of the killing to Lizzie which were inaccurate. He told her Rachel had been raped, when she had not, and incorrectly described the position of her body. 'Dr Britton pulled the strings,' said the judge. 'This was a desperately lonely young man, a sexual virgin, longing for a relationship. I am certain Lizzie James played upon that loneliness and those aspirations.'

From the start of the undercover operation in mid-January 1993 until May the same year, nothing emerged from the correspondence between Stagg and Lizzie which matched the psychologist's profile, he said. From then on the fantasy content became progessively more extreme. 'I accept that the increasingly extreme fantasies were the product of deliberate shaping by the policewoman. She was deliberately deceiving him by encouraging him to express his fantasies because she enjoyed them and the more extreme the better.' A key letter, he said, was the one in which she had said, 'Each time you write I know we get closer and closer. You seem so much like me. I hope we can be soul mates. They [the letters] excite me greatly, but I cannot help but think you are showing great restraint. You are showing control when you feel like bursting — I want you to burst. I want to feel you all powerful and overwhelming so that I am completely in your power, defenceless and humiliated. These letters are sending me into paradise already.'

Another indication of Lizzie's manipulation, he said, was the letter in which she wrote, 'My fantasies know no bounds and my imagination runs riot . . . sometimes I scare myself with what I really want. Sometimes normal things are just not enough — not just straight sex.' They were words familiar to those involved in the trial; soon they were to be revealed to the public at large as the press corps tensed to send the Ognall judgment across the world. There was no other way the decision could go now — Stagg was about to walk free. However, His Lordship had not finished yet.

Stagg, he said, had talked during the latter part of the operation about slashing a woman's neck during sexual intercourse. This was highly relevant, he said, because Rachel had been stabbed 49 times. 'Lizzie James,' said the judge, 'taped a cassette of fantasies for Stagg. It is a highly explicit tape covering male domination, group sex and the use of a knife by a man to heighten sexual excitement. It is scarcely surprising that, thereafter, the accused continues to speak of a knife in relation to a sexual incident.'

He said it was hard to accept the prosecution's claim that Lizzie James had only asked direct questions about the murder when it was necessary to do so to preserve her cover. Her secretly recorded meetings with Stagg, four in all in Hyde Park, had shown a 'consistent attempt' to elicit a confession from Stagg, saying that without it the relationship would have to end. 'This serves to demonstrate the lengths to which the officer was prepared to go in this operation,' he said. The rules covering entrapment, he went on, were the same where a suspect is tricked into providing evidence, such as fingerprints, as they were for someone providing material for an offender profile.

The judge then ruled that all the evidence gathered in the undercover operation would be inadmissible and said he would not consider separating the section dealing with the 'prayer-like' position of Rachel's hands, which the prosecution had submitted would be relevant and admissible on its own. 'I do not accept that this material could be construed as a confession,' he said, 'and it is so flimsy that prejudice exceeds its probative value.'

John Nutting who, as senior treasury counsel, is one of Britain's foremost prosecution barristers, rose quickly to his feet as soon as the judge had finished his ruling. The Crown, he said, were now right back to where they were in September 1992 after Stagg's first arrest when the Crown Prosecution Service had decided there was insufficient evidence to proceed with a murder charge against him. In the absence of the Lizzie James testimony, he said, the Crown would offer no further evidence and a verdict of not guilty should be entered. The judge duly directed, at exactly 11:45 a.m. on 14 September 1994, that Colin Stagg should now walk free. A thin smile flickered across Stagg's face as the decision prompted a burst of shouting and cheering from the public gallery. 'See you outside, Colin,' shouted one of his brothers. Stagg turned to wave at his mother and she smiled back, her eyes watering with tears of relief.

Below her, Monica Nickell was weeping for another reason. For her, the agony of her daughter's tragic death would go on for many years to come. She clung tightly to her husband's arm. Son Mark, looking distressed, gave what consolation he could. They had half expected this and Andrew had a statement ready written.

Jostling had begun. People's emotions were flooding among the crush of people in the street outside. Police horses were needed to protect this quiet and reserved family, so bitterly wounded by the never-ending tragedy, from the flashing cameras, intrusive microphones, inquiring voices and the sheer weight of the media pack wanting to know how they felt now. What could they possibly say?

They were escorted from the surge to an island in the middle of the road where Andrew Nickell pulled his statement from his pocket and began competing with the traffic to be heard. With Monica clutching his arm and more tears never far away, Andrew's words came from the heart, surprisingly loud and clear, rehearsed, no doubt, a hundred times in his mind for this moment that he had dreaded.

'When my daughter was murdered I believed, like many other citizens, that the law was even-handed and that justice was available to all. I am afraid the last two and a quarter years have been a period of disillusionment. What appears to have been lost over the last 30 years is the principle that everyone is equal under law. The pendulum has swung too far to the side of the criminal. Why has this situation arisen when society seems to care more for the criminal and less for the victim and their families? When is society and government going to redress the balance so that the scales of justice are level?'

Standing just at the back of the crowd, Mike Wickerson and Keith Pedder plainly shared this sense of frustration. Andrew Nickell continued:

'At this point I want to pay a tribute to the bravery of the undercover policewoman who put her life on the line. At the end of the operation, the police, the psychologist and the Crown Prosecution Service all had their own views as to whether Stagg was the murderer.

Thirteen months later, having been committed for trial, Stagg now walks free. He has not been tried by a jury. His Lordship, Mr Justice Ognall, ruled that the police undercover operation broke the rules laid down to ensure a safe conviction. The ruling is well argued in law and guided by many a precedent. The effect, however, is to rule that all the evidence gained during the undercover operation is inadmissible in a court of law. The law has been upheld, but where is the justice?'

Mr Nickell made a significant pause to reinforce his point. 'I understand that the police will now keep the file on my daughter's murder open,' he went on. 'They are not looking for anyone else.' This was the phrase that disappointed police officers had used so many times in the past to indicate their concern over a court decision but under new guidelines, they are no longer allowed to say anything. 'We have an impasse,' said Andrew Nickell, 'which may, and I emphasise may, put other daughters and wives at risk in the months and years ahead.' The imbalance in the law, he said, allowed a defendant to stay silent during a trial without any significance being drawn to the fact. 'The whole of the evidence in this case,' he said, 'I believe ten thousand pages, is given to the defence for them to study and to find an answer. The defence must give the prosecution nothing until the trial commences. The prosecution have no appeal whatsoever against today's decision. If it was the other way round then Colin Stagg's lawyers could have taken his case to the Court of Appeal . . . If the defence has the right of appeal why not let the case be heard by a jury and not stifle the evidence? At every stage it seems the defendant has the advantage. We, as a society, require fairness for all, not just for the criminal.'

There was one little boy in all this, said Andrew Nickell, who needs the protection of us all, his little grandson Alex, so far away from all this in the south of France. Monica gripped her husband's arm a little tighter and brushed a tear from her eye as he continued:

'He is the two-year-old boy who clung to my daughter while the killer murdered her in the most foul way. He will spend the rest of his life remembering those dreadful moments. He and his father have, with enormous courage, made a start in another country. They have survived but Alex remembers everything that happened. Alex's one hope is that you leave him alone in the peace and security he needs to grow up without the constant fear of being discovered by the media. Leave him in peace; he deserves that chance. Do not publish his photo, don't seek him out, please; leave him alone. I think that society and the law owe him some justice.'

It was a sentiment with which no-one could possibly disagree.

The true identity of Lizzie James will remain a secret for ever. The judge ordered that it must never be published in order to protect her future activities in the dangerous world of undercover operations. He agreed to her future anonymity after reading a personal letter from the Yard expert whose men had protected her during Operation Edzell, Commander Roy Ramm of the SO10 surveillance unit.

Having collected his personal belongings from the cells and handed them to his family to look after, Colin Stagg emerged fifteen minutes later, after Mr and Mrs Nickell and Mark had left all the chaos and emotional confusion behind them, to return home to Ampthill with their memories. Looking tiny, Stagg came out holding a typed statement. Flanked by his successful legal team, with dozens of copies to hand to the press, he stood close to the Old Bailey wall, near where an IRA bomb went off in 1973, to deliver a bitter message to the world. His voice barely audible in the crush, he was dwarfed by the camera teams as he spoke. 'I am innocent and I have always been innocent of this horrible crime and I am pleased that this has finally been proved. I hope now the police will go out and find the real killer . . .' then he couldn't help the anger flowing as he left his prepared script and added, 'the fat, lazy bastards'. His year inside, he said, had been a nightmare.

'I have gone through a lot of emotional and physical stress. So much, in fact, that the thought of taking my own life was never far from my mind. My life has been ruined by a mixture of half-baked psychological theories and some stories written to satisfy the strange sexual requests of an undercover police officer. The judge recognised that there was never any evidence against me, no forensic evidence, no confession evidence, nothing at all. I now intend to take proceedings against the police and the psychologist Mr Paul Britton for the anguish and distress that I have suffered during the last thirteen months in prison. I hope now the press will allow me some privacy over the next few days as I recover from my ordeal and I am reunited with my dog Brandy.'

He signed off by thanking his legal team for their belief in his innocence and for their strength in fighting his case. By now one of the legal team had commandeered a London taxi and was waiting close by to whisk Stagg away from the crowds. He was taken to a four-star London hotel for interviews with ITN and the BBC and his first meal outside a prison canteen for more than a year. He was smiling a lot by now . . .

He was on TV that night, telling how he had fallen for Lizzie James 'hook, line and sinker' and felt utterly betrayed when she finally revealed her true identity. ITN reporter Joan Thirkettle had been convinced of Stagg's innocence for a long while and was never afraid to express her views. She had formed a sympathetic relationship with Hilda and David Carr. Stagg, now 31 years old, was asked directly if he had killed Rachel. 'No, I did not,' he said firmly in a news bulletin that reached millions across Britain. 'A crime like this is a crime against God, against the universe itself. I believe all life is sacred, from insects to human beings.' Of Rachel's distraught family he said, 'I feel very sorry for them and very sad for them because they were seeing a man who was obviously set up by the police when they should have been seeing the real murderer.' On Newsroom South East, his message to the Nickells was: 'Don't be angry with me. Be angry with the police who set me up and let the real murderer go free.' Next morning he was back on the television screen tucking into a full English breakfast of the type that Wandsworth doesn't serve, scanning the morning papers and again protesting his total innocence of the Rachel murder.

Meanwhile, Andrew Nickell was on GMTV giving his whole-hearted support to the police team.

'People will listen to me and say, "OK he will be biased," because we have obviously been close to the police over the last two years and quite frankly they have been magnificent. Given the circumstances where someone was arrested, he was then freed but they were still quite convinced that person was guilty, I don't see what else they were supposed to do. Are they supposed to walk away and leave society in some danger? They went to the Crown Prosecution Service, they took legal advice, as I understand it, at every stage of the operation. And yet they go to the Old Bailey and get it absolutely slaughtered. Why? They are trying to do their jobs. All I can say is that I know nothing about the law, I'm concerned about trying to find my daughter's murderer and keeping society safe. There are times I listened to the evidence and said, "Well, was there another way?" but I don't see there was another way. How were they supposed to do it? All the time, society want the police to protect them. We put one hand behind their back. We blindfold them and we don't support them in any way. And yet every time something goes wrong we criticise the police. It is very easy for a judge to sit at the Old Bailey in dry surroundings when he's had a week to consider what he wants to say. He's not out there on the streets. He is not on Wimbledon Common picking up someone's body which has been cut. He's not picking somebody out of a car. They are the people who are trying to keep society safe for us and all the time we legislate against them, we make it more and more difficult for them to do their job.'

Monica spoke movingly about her little grandson, now living in a tiny French village where the locals think his mother died in a car crash, saying,

'He talks about Rachel now. He didn't for about a year. He has pictures of her everywhere and says, "This is my mummy". In the summer he came to stay with me and I took him swimming. He said, "Have we been to this pool before?" and I said yes, we went there with Mummy. He said, "I can remember what Mummy looks like, but I can't remember what she feels like" and from a small boy that is quite a sad thing to hear him say. But I understand that feeling because I almost forget what she feels like.'

Commenting on speculation that Stagg could reap a fortune in compensation and newspaper deals, Andrew added, 'What value society puts on people is incomprehensible.' He said a provisional offer to Alex from the Criminal Injuries Compensation Board had worked out at £22,000 or seventeen pence an hour until he is eighteen.

That day's tabloids carried particularly unflattering pictures of Stagg on their front pages. 'Now I'll Make a Killing', said the *Daily Mirror* headline, referring to the bonanza payout Stagg was now hoping for from Scotland Yard. 'No Girl is Safe' proclaimed *The Sun*'s monster headline sandwiched between a photo of Stagg and one of Rachel. They said the 'mystery sex beast' who had murdered Rachel was now 'laughing at the law amid fears that he will kill again'. The *Daily Express* asked simply, 'Where is the Justice?', echoing the words of Andrew Nickell. The *Times* said straightforwardly, 'Judge Attacks Police Over "Murder Trap" ' and showed Stagg emerging a free man from the Old Bailey with solicitor Ian Ryan and barrister Jim Sturman at his side. The *Daily Mail* carried a photograph of little Alex as a baby, romping with Rachel beside the headline 'The Child Who Still Waits for Justice'. They quoted tormented Andre Hanscombe as saying, 'I can't believe it. The nightmare goes on.' He said he was appalled at the inconclusive end to the murder which had so damaged his life. 'I feel so much anger; and I have two and a half years of anger inside me,' he said. 'It's one blow after another. Where's the justice? Where's the sense? It's difficult to know how to go on. It's a neverending source of pain.' He and his bonny son, now five, were left to comfort each other in the quiet of their French hideaway.

The Old Bailey decision generated a massive reaction over the length and breadth of the country, which was to rumble on for weeks. If Colin Stagg sued, how much would he expect to get? Would he be granted legal aid to challenge the police? Speculation ranged from Stagg expecting to pocket from £60,000 to a massive £225,000, based on known compensation figures in cases of alleged unlawful arrest. His solicitor was hawking Stagg's inside story of the arrest, with full details of his honey-trap affair with Lizzie James, for 'around fifty grand'. There was no immediate rush to sign him up, but rumours grew of a deal with the *News of the World* which would involve Stagg taking a lie detector test.

Many papers were quick to seize on the huge disparity between Alex's probable payout for the loss of his radiant young mother — the maximum that could be allotted — and the amount Stagg might collect. It prompted a fiery broadside at the legal system from the *Daily Star* in a front-page editorial headed 'It Stinks'. The paper said the case had been rightly booted out of court but asked, 'Why should a convicted flasher; a misfit who could not hold down a full-time job, a creature who lurked in a sordid flat plastered with satanic symbols and boasted in kinky letters of committing acts of self-abuse on Wimbledon Common . . . why should such a disgusting excuse for a man grow rich because he spent thirteen months in custody? Would he have put that time to better use? A quarter of a million pounds' worth of better use?'

The inquest into what went wrong and who was to blame saw Scotland Yard Commissioner, Sir Paul Condon, and the Director of Public Prosecutions, Barbara Mills, standing firmly by their decision to prosecute Colin Stagg. Sir Paul promised a thorough review of the investigation by a senior and highly experienced officer. Privately, the detectives involved in the Rachel inquiry were bitter at the way they had been portrayed as Machiavellian mischief makers trying to stitch up Colin Stagg. They feared nothing from an official inquiry into the way the case was handled. Things might have been different, they said, if only a judge and jury had heard the rest of the evidence they had planned to submit; if it had not all boiled down to the legal rights and wrongs of the Lizzie James testimony. 'If a jury had acquitted Colin Stagg after hearing all the evidence, then we would have had no complaints,' said one officer, 'but to see the case shot down in flames before a jury was even sworn was a dreadful blow.'

The beleaguered police team got quick reassurance from Sir Paul Condon that he stood squarely behind their actions. I feel no sense of shame or embarrassment at what was done,' he said. The Commissioner, returning from a trip abroad to find his officers facing a huge barrage of criticism, issued a statement saying:

'I have decided to comment because I feel the people of London should hear from me personally. I do not believe that my officers acted improperly or outside the law in the way they conducted the investigation, or afterwards. What do we do in circumstances where a victim has been murdered? Surely we have a public duty, in the public interest, to explore and test every legitimate avenue of evidence. The reason we embarked on this undercover operation was to try to do that. It was never our intention that the undercover operation should be the centrepiece of our evidence. It was always our ambition to find forensic and other detailed evidence. This was not achieved, but what did result from that operation was very properly exposed to the most exhaustive legal filters which exist in this country. The CPS had obtained independent Treasury Counsel advice who advised that in the public interest the matter should be put before a court. But, even more important, the evidence was subjected to the ultimate legal filter before a trial takes place — a contested committal. A stipendiary magistrate said, "This case far from limps past a prima facie stage." An individual judge has now taken a view of the case we must respect. We will study very carefully what he said, we are always prepared to learn lessons. But what I must say is that we had a woman officer who, with a very strong sense of public duty, acted out a part in the most difficult circumstances imaginable. She deserves, and has, my thanks. Throughout the case we have acted in the public interest and we have exposed every single thing we have done to the appropriate legal authorities. And I would like to say the CPS have given us quite excellent support throughout.'

The Commissioner's statement seemed effectively to nail the lie in some of the heavier papers of a massive buck-passing bust-up between the police and the CPS. The Wimbledon team were always adamant that they had been on the same side throughout the investigation and each had respected the views of the other. There had not been some sort of running battle.

On the day of his release, Stagg's friend and neighbour Cheryl Lewis revealed that she had warned him the Lizzie letters were a police trap. She said Stagg had read her the first letter from Lizzie and she had told him, 'That's the police — they are trying to trap you.' She said, 'It was so obvious. It started off with: "Hi Colin, you don't know me but I was staying with Julie and read a letter you sent her. You sound like my type of guy." Colin said he didn't know a Julie — anyone with any sense could have seen it was from the police and I told him so. In her second letter, Lizzie said she had sold her flat and moved into a hotel and he should send her letters there. I told Colin he was mad to get involved when it was obviously some sort of set-up.' Stagg later send a letter to Cheryl from Wandsworth jail, saying, 'I should have listened to you. You said it could be a trap.'

Four days after Stagg's acquittal — and with debate still raging over the case — the *News of the World* revealed that he had taken a lie detector test at their invitation and it had proclaimed him not guilty of the Rachel murder, despite the 'huge cloud of suspicion' which still hung over him. The polygraph results, said the paper, showed that Stagg was certainly sexually disturbed. 'But they clear him — almost beyond doubt — of any involvement in Rachel's murder.' Reporters Neville Thurlbeck — who had worked on the Stagg case while he was with *Today* newspaper and had built up a rapport with the family — and crime man Gary Jones wrote, 'These results provide an emphatic answer to the question all Britain has been asking: "Did he do it?" And they will be a further blow to the police team who were convinced they had their man.'

They said Stagg had undergone a lie detector test supervised by Jeremy Barratt, Britain's foremost polygraph expert, who had posed fifteen key questions relating to Rachel's killing and Stagg's movements on that day. 'Have you masturbated on Wimbledon Common?'

'Yes.'

'Did you ever see Rachel Nickell alive?'

'No.'

'Did you kill Rachel Nickell?'

'No.'

'Is it possible Rachel Nickell ever saw you masturbate?'

'No.'

Stagg's responses, said the paper, were the same to simple questions like: 'Is your name Colin?' as they were to the crunch questions over Rachel's death. The needles on the polygraph 'didn't even flicker' said the paper's headlines. They quoted one of Scotland Yard's most respected former officers, ex-Flying Squad chief John O'Connor, as saying, 'The results in this test would suggest that consideration be given to this inquiry being reopened with a view to looking for an entirely different suspect.'

Not surprisingly, the Wimbledon team were unimpressed. Commissioner Condon said disparagingly, 'We live in the real world. This is not some sort of television drama.'

Stagg was now saying that he didn't blame the police for suspecting him of murdering Rachel. 'I know I seem like a low life, so I understand why the police tried to nail me,' he said. 'I let my sexual fantasies run riot, but I never put those fantasies into practice.' He revealed that new girlfriend Diane Rooney had finally taken the virginity he had been so desperate to lose when they shared a night of passion at the Waldorf after walking to freedom from the Old Bailey. Stagg said he was planning to start a new life with Diane, free, he hoped, from the shadow of the Wimbledon Common murder. Diane, a 26-year-old care-worker who befriended Stagg by writing to him in jail after his arrest, said she hoped to move into his Roehampton maisonette, pagan symbols and all. 'Ours is just a normal relationship,' said Stagg, cuddling up to buxom Diane on a hotel settee.

The same day the *News of the World* 'cleared' Stagg,

the *Mail on Sunday* and its authoritative crime correspondent Chester Stern disclosed that Scotland Yard would strongly resist any claim for compensation in a civil court and would be prepared to produce all their evidence — material banned from the Old Bailey plus everything else in their files — in what would amount to a new 'trial' for Colin Stagg. Where no criminal charges are involved, the police would be permitted to put Lizzie James and any other witnesses in the witness box. A civil action would not be about Stagg's guilt or innocence but about whether the police were justified in hauling him in as their prime suspect, that they had not brought a malicious prosecution against him. Stagg's reputation would stand or fall, said Stern, former head of Scotland Yard's Press Bureau, on how much a jury decided to award him in damages.

The Rachel Nickell case will go down in the annals of criminal investigations as one of the most horrific, perplexing and frustrating that any police force has ever tackled. It will surely haunt Andrew and Monica Nickell and Andre Hanscombe and young Alex for the rest of their lives. The shadow over Colin Stagg will only be lifted, in the public's eyes, if and when another suspect is arrested, charged and convicted. The questions still of paramount importance to every decent human being in Britain are: 'Who did kill Rachel Nickell? Where is he now? Will he ever strike again?'

On that pleasant common where Rachel died so cruelly that summer morning, normality has returned. The grey squirrels scamper among the trees, the crows and jackdaws squawk for titbits from passing walkers, joggers and riders share breathless exercise. The silver birch under which Rachel's body was so callously abandoned by her killer is dead. The oak nearby, which became known as her memorial tree, where hundreds left bouquets and wreaths, spreads its boughs and thrives.

Looking at the twin-pronged trunk of the slowly decaying birch from the spot where Rachel strolled just seconds before her death, the branches look like a ghostly pair of antlers reaching up to the heavens.

And the detectives from Wimbledon police station still go there from time to time, watching, waiting, hoping for an answer.

THE MURDER OF RACHEL NICKELL
The truth about the tragic murder on Wimbledon Common
Mike Fielder

CAGED HEAT
What really goes on behind the bars of women's prisons
Wensley Clarkson

KNIGHTSBRIDGE: THE ROBBERY OF THE CENTURY
The dramatic story of one of the world's most notorious crimes
Valerio Viccei

BROTHERS IN BLOOD
The horrific story of two brothers who murdered their own parents
Tom Brown and Paul Cheston

YOU COULD WIN THE AMAZING SLEUTH'S SILVER DAGGER!

The first twelve titles in Blake's True Crime Library series each contain a question relating to the book. Collect the numbered editions of Blake's True Crime Library, and when you have the answers to all the questions, fill in the form which you will find at the back of the twelfth book and send it to Blake Publishing to be entered into a prize draw.

HERE IS THE TENTH QUESTION
With which religion was Colin Stagg involved?
The winner will receive the exclusive sleuth's silver dagger and five runners-up will receive three free copies of Blake's True Crime Library titles.

How To Enter
Fill in the answer form contained in the twelfth book in the series and post it to us. If you have won, we will notify you. Whether you are a winner or not, you will still be eligible for a *FREE* True Crime newsletter!

Competition Rules
1.   The 'How to Enter' instructions form part of the rules.
2.   These competitions are not open to any members of Blake Publishing or their families, or Blake Publishing's advertising agents, printers or distributors.
3.   The prizes will be awarded in order of their value, to the senders of the first winning entries after the closing date.
4.   Entries must be on the entry coupon supplied and will not be accepted after the closing date.
5.   No claim is necessary, winners will be notified.
6.   In cases where a manufacturer discontinues a product which has been specified as a prize, Blake Publishing Ltd will substitute the nearest equivalent model of similar or higher value.
7.   The Editor's decision is final, and no correspondence can be entered into.

BEAT THE RUSH!
ORDER YOUR COPIES OF FORTHCOMING TRUE CRIME TITLES DIRECTLY.

Simply fill in the form below, and we will send you your books as they become available.

Name: ....

Address: ....

....

....

Daytime tel.: ....

Card (please tick as appropriate)

Visa ☐ Mastercard ☐

Access ☐ Switch ☐

Card number: ....

Expiry date: ....

For Switch cards only:

Issue date .... Issue number ....

Please send me (tick as appropriate)

☐ Deadlier than the Male
Wensley Clarkson

☐ Natural Born Killers
Kate Kray

☐ In the Company of Killers
Norman Parker

☐ The Spanish Connection
John Lightfoot

☐ Doctors who Kill
Wensley Clarkson

☐ Deadly Affair
Nicholas Davies

☐ Female of the Species
Wensley Clarkson

☐ Women in Chains
Wensley Clarkson

☐ Caged Heat
Wensley Clarkson

☐ Knightsbridge: Robbery of the Century
Valerio Viccei

☐ Brothers in Blood
Tom Brown and Paul Cheston

All titles are £4.99. Postage and packing are free. No money will be deducted from your card until the books become available.